TENDING THE FIRE

Studies in Art,
Therapy
and Creativity

To Gabriel and Jesse,
two of the most creative people I know...

TENDING THE FIRE

Studies in Art,
Therapy
and Creativity

Ellen Levine

PALMERSTON PRESS Toronto

Palmerston Press

© **1995 Ellen Levine**

Published by Palmerston Press
822 Manning Avenue
Toronto, Ontario M6G 2W8
Tel. (416) 516-2644
Fax. (416) 516-2067

ISBN 1-895450-74-8

Printed and Bound in Canada

Printed by Ryerson Printing House

Palmerston Press

Cover Painting by Ellen Levine, "Burning Land," 1994.

Contents

Acknowledgments

Writing a book requires a solitary and single-minded attitude. It can be experienced as a lonely endeavor which takes one away from the world. Although the act of writing has been solitary for me, I have experienced intense forms of connection during the course of the whole project. First, it has brought me into deeper connection with myself through thinking about my work over the last twenty years and through the painting process which sparked the book and set the project on fire. It has also brought me into connection with others and into the experience of a global community that has provided support, stimulation, and encouragement for my work. This community consists of many of my friends and colleagues in the field— Steve Levine, Paolo Knill, Shaun McNiff, Elizabeth McKim, Margot Fuchs, Yaacov Naor, Annette Brederode, Majken Jacoby, Gunda Graenicher, Geoffrey Scott-Alexander, Jack Weller, Peter and Brigitte Wanzenreid. Fellow travellers and fire builders. Students, too, have been part of my community and have given me a great deal in terms of understanding the work of expressive arts therapy by continuing to question and to probe.

I would like to express particular appreciation to the staff of ISIS-Canada, Fran Harwood, Audra McManus and Agnes Struik, and to my colleagues at the C.M. Hincks Centre for Children's Mental Health, particularly Art Caspary, Brent Willock and

Elsa Broder. Without their willingness to take over for me while I went off to write, this project would never have happened.

Steve Levine, my husband, partner, colleague and friend was instrumental in this project. He had a way of understanding what I was doing here almost before I realized it. His editorial work brought the essence of my writing to the forefront and crystallized the ideas into a tight, focused whole. I especially acknowledge him here as an incredible midwife for this project. I look forward to reading more of his own work as it emerges over the next few years.

Some of the material which appears in this book was published elsewhere in slightly different form: "Women and Creativity: Art-In-Relationship," in *The Arts in Psychotherapy*, Vol. 16, Number 4, Winter, 1989, and "Playing with Fire: Reflections on the Ethics of Expressive Arts Therapy," in *C.R.E.A.T.E.: Journal of the Creative and Expressive Arts Therapy Exchange*, Volume 5, 1995.

Finally, thanks go to my publisher, Colleen Perrin, whose attitude toward this endeavour has always been positive and forward-looking.

Foreword

Tending the fire is an exciting task: it can go dead, it can blaze out of control, it can burst forth in a sudden blaze, it can be a bouquet of singular sparks. Simple warmth, if not properly tended, can become an inferno. Aggression and love in one container. A bonfire of oppositions: solitude and connection, freedom and confinement, merger and separation, defense and vulnerability, questions and questings, theory and practice, formlessness and shape, participation and interpretation.

In her book, *Tending the Fire: Studies in Art, Therapy, and Creativity,* Ellen Levine prepares an inclusive place for people to be makers, and she is careful to guard the space so one can enter trustfully. She enters herself. She closes the door. She opens the door. She turns and returns to the fire she tends. She holds the child freely, and the child begins to dance. Together, they sing a fire out of a storm. They *name* what they have experienced. She is patient and present for others; attending, she knows how to nurture herself as she moves through over/layers and under/pinnings of meaning and image. She is an artist among others, and, as she travels, she paints her journey alive.

Ellen Levine allows us to know those who informed her and provided her with a solid psychoanalytic grounding to which she can return; at the same time, she continues in her own explorations, not knowing where her journey will lead her. She acknowledges her colleagues and fellow travellers in the field of expressive arts therapy, and she adds her voice to others growing stronger in the gathering fire. In her tending, she weaves reflecting and changing colors and forms, textures and images. Sometimes she is still and listening. Sometimes she struggles. Sometimes she is both student and teacher at the same time. Sometimes she tosses and turns in consternation and resistance. Sometimes she dances.

In her care/full way, Ellen Levine does not lose sight of the theory underlying the work, and weaves its orange strands through the entire book, which is, for now, her transitional space. The healing power of play, the entry into chaos, the search for authentic symbolic language through the making of art, the need for naming one's experience and the longing for order are all part of the integrity of the whole. As we travel with her, we begin to understand more fully her practice with women, with early adolescents, her own image-making, her scholarship, her questions, and her primary and abiding relationships to those she loves, to those she learns from, and to those communities in which she belongs. The flames grow more diverse and more enduring in their changing.

In *Tending the Fire,* we are allowed to see journeywoman: artist: wife: mother: clinician: therapist: colleague: a real person with dilemmas and delights, longings and homing instincts, using and reusing the "stuff of tending" to make her creation: this work, this play, this other, this book. Welcome Ellen Levine's book into your self. It will tend you well.

Elizabeth Gordon McKim: Poet

Bali, February, 1995

Fire is the ultra-living element. It is intimate and it is universal. It lives in our heart. It lives in the sky. It rises from the depths of the substance and offers itself with the warmth of love. Or it can go back down into the substance and hide there, latent and pent-up, like hate and vengeance. Among all phenomena, it is really the only one to which there can be so definitely attributed the opposing values of good and evil. It shines in Paradise. It burns in Hell. It is gentleness and torture. It is cookery and it is apocalypse. It is a pleasure for the *good* child sitting prudently by the hearth; yet it punishes any disobedience when the child wishes to play too close to its flames. It is well-being and it is respect. It is a tutelary and a terrible divinity, both good and bad. It can contradict itself; thus it is one of the principles of universal explanation.

Gaston Bachelard, *The Psychoanalysis of Fire*

Introduction

With the publication of this book, I add my voice to the chorus of my colleagues who have been thinking and writing about the newly emerging field of expressive arts therapy for the last few years. Our field is beginning to grow and to acquire a body of literature. We have been practicing as therapists and training others to practice. Now some of us are setting down our thoughts and developing guiding principles. What I have always appreciated about the spirit of our work is the fact that we approach it from many different perspectives. We hold together in this literature a wide variety of voices and attitudes. It is in the nature of expressive arts therapy to be multi-modal, distinguishing itself from the more traditional specializations such as art therapy, dance therapy, music therapy, drama or poetry therapy. This multiplicity reflects the multi-modal nature of the arts themselves and also mirrors the capacity of our work to hold the tension of opposites and differences.

These varied voices include, for example, the work of Shaun McNiff who has been writing about the arts in therapy since the early 1970's. His direction has been to develop a depth psychology of art which takes account of the need which psyche has to manifest itself in the form of images. How we invite these images to come forward and how we treat them is essential in our work. In his recent book, *Art as Medicine* (1992),

McNiff states that pathology is "...essential to the ecosystem of the soul." The images of art and of dreams express soul in all of its manifestations. This idea of images as messengers or angels of the soul in its deep aspects requires that we develop a way to work with the images that does justice to them. Accordingly, McNiff has followed James Hillman's practice of *staying with the image:*

> It means staying with the medium, the process, and the artistic discipline, whether it be drama, movement, poetry, music, or painting. "Sticking with the image" includes staying with sounds, gestures, body movements, feelings, environments, and other aspects of art forms. When we leave the image, we leave the context and the presence of soul (McNiff, 1992, p. 55).

Keeping the images flowing and alive is essential to this way of working. McNiff has also contributed the method of *dialoguing with images*: a way of listening to the images rather than an attempt to explain them or talk about them. Akin to the process of free association in psychoanalytic practice, the dialogue is a form of poetic speech which treats the image or images in a work of art as if they were living beings capable of informing us about themselves. This way of approaching images, which I will discuss further in this book, retains their freshness and spontaneity as well as their depth.

Another voice in the multiplicity of perspectives which comprises our current literature is the work of Stephen K. Levine in his book, *Poiesis: The Language of Psychology and the Speech of the Soul* (1992). What Levine contributes that is unique is his vision of a philosophical context for the emergence and the practice of expressive arts therapy. Rather than speak about method or technique, Levine shows how the interdisciplinary approach of the integration of the arts fits with the philosophical tradition of Kant and Heidegger amongst others who stress the importance of the multiplicity of appearances contained within the creative imagination. Although we aspire to wholeness and integration, the need to experiment with new forms by breaking up the old ones is fundamental to human experience and fundamental to the nature of the creative act. In criticizing the tendency for the arts therapies to become specialized and reified in therapeutic practice, Levine wants us to be asking larger questions about the foundations of our work. In addressing the basic question of what it means to be human, Levine focuses on the imagination. It is in the imagination, in the realm of creativity, that our essential and authentic relationship to the world is to be found. Here he cites Heidegger's notion of *poiesis* as central:

> When we ask what kind of existence is authentic existence, Heidegger's ultimate answer is that it is "poetic" existence. He is referring here not primarily to poetry in the sense of written verse but to poetry as the imaginative capacity for envisioning and speaking one's own authentic truth....Poiesis is that act by which truth is placed in a work; it is the casting forward of new possibilities of being-in-the-world which are then held or contained in an art-work (Levine, 1992, p. 36).

To Heidegger's work, Levine joins the perspective of D.W. Winnicott who makes the connection between creativity as essential to human aliveness and the work of therapy. For Winnicott, the work of therapy is to foster creative expression in the patient, to play with the patient in a therapeutic manner. As expressive arts therapists, because we work and play with the stuff of imagination and use the container of the arts to carry forward the work of imagination in therapy, addressing these ultimate questions is crucial for our work. In terms of Levine's perspective, our work is better informed and grounded when we pay attention to the broader, more ultimate context within which we are situated.

Paolo Knill has been pioneering an approach to the understanding of the project of expressive arts therapy for many years. His work, in North America and in Europe, has provided a sense of excitement and rich possibility for us and has added yet another perspective to our practice and now to our literature: the aesthetic foundations of the discipline of the arts. Knill, co-author of a new book, *Minstrels of Soul: Intermodal Expressive Therapy* (1995), develops a set of first principles for intermodal work in expressive therapy which is articulated finally for English speaking readers.

Like McNiff and Levine, imagination is central for Knill. It is, in and of itself, intermodal. Knill uses two theoretical frameworks to approach an understanding of the multiplicity of imagination: polyaesthetics and crystallization theory. Polyaesthetics understands the arts as implicitly distinct and differentiated yet interconnected by their very nature as communicative and based in the senses. Crystallization theory takes account of the human tendency to integrate and unite disparate elements, "...[moving] towards optimal clarity and precision of feeling and thought" (Knill, et. al., 1995, p. 28). This is the double movement that informs intermodal expressive arts therapy: the working with differentiation and multiplicity of expression in a variety of media and art forms and the pull to crystallize or purify expression into a clear, sharp and sensitive whole.

Love and aggression play significant roles in the work of expressive arts therapy. Knill is unique in paying close attention to these aspects of human experience as they enter the therapeutic space and as they are addressed and help to transform the self through the artistic process. The imaginal realm is essentially erotic and soul moves within this realm. For Knill, work with imagination and the arts is soul-making activity and, in this way, essentially involves us with love in all of its forms. Likewise, aggression is there. In making anything in the arts, an act of tearing down is necessary. This is not destruction but, rather, a *destructuring* where substances are transformed and something new emerges from the bits and pieces of the old form. As therapists, it is essential that we are capable of holding the aggression and allowing it to find its proper form and shape in the container of the arts.

The notion of aesthetic response and response-ability are key in the development of intermodal expressive work for Knill. Here he is speaking about what happens when we work with the stuff of imagination: we train ourselves to be acutely *sensitive* so that we can foster depth and sensitivity in the people with whom we work and, thus, invite imagination to flower. In this way, beauty enters our work. We are involved in responding to the presence of beauty whose form may be pleasing or disturbing, but it must *move* us nevertheless.

The work of Natalie Rogers fits as well into the multiplicity of perspectives that is currently developing in our field. In her book, *The Creative Connection: Expressive Arts as Healing* (1994), Rogers delineates her "person-centred" approach to expressive therapy which involves an adaptation of Carl Rogers' "client-centred" therapy to the use of the arts in therapy. Here one follows the client's lead in moving into the use of art materials, akin to McNiff's emphasis upon staying with the image and letting it speak to us. The therapist is a receptive facilitator of process. Rogers emphasizes the importance of process over product, in contrast to Knill who suggests that we need to pay more attention to art-making in and of itself and to developing an acute *aesthetic* awareness of the impact of our activity on ourselves and others.

In her book, Rogers develops and employs the concept of the "creative connection." For her, the interplay amongst the different art modalities stimulates self-exploration. Going inside by means of the arts, expressing feelings out of the "deep well" of the unconscious in the form of the art-work and moving back out into the world is the rhythm of therapy with the arts. One begins in a particular form of art and then is lead to incorporate other forms, spiralling downward and releasing layers of inhibition. Making art is the vehicle to explore inner life and to effect release through insight about what has been made.

Finally, I would like to mention the work of Arthur Robbins who was one of the first creative arts therapists to incorporate the perspective of object relations theory which I also draw upon in this book. In *The Artist as Therapist* (1987) and other works, Robbins has explored the connection between expressive arts therapy and psychoanalysis which I feel gives theoretical depth to our practical work.

What then am I adding to this multiplicity of perspectives which are diverse, on the one hand, and interconnected on the other? What I hope to explore in this book is the notion of creativity as an internal sense of vitality which emerges as we enter the world and then is either enhanced or diminished by the experiences that we have throughout our lives. My perspective comes from practicing therapy mainly with children and seeing how the arts provide an essential oasis space for them to play and, in a fundamental sense, to be. In the work that I have done with adults, I have seen how helping them to reconnect with the lost or diminished creative source has rippled out to other aspects of life and served to enliven their experience.

My perspective also comes from teaching and training students to do the work of expressive arts therapy out in the community in a wide variety of settings, from schools to treatment centers to nursing homes and hospitals. I have felt that people "out there" are hungry for the work that we do. Because we are working to stimulate imagination and use play and spontaneous art-making to achieve this kind of stimulation, there is the sense that our work itself is playful. While it can be fun, what is also happening is that, in the process of making art, soul is being engaged, the self is enlivened and deep expression comes forward. This may often involve intense emotion and put people in touch with painful feelings.   The arts help to provide a container for these experiences and, because of this, create enough of a balance between risk and safety so that this deepening can happen. Student training groups are also working on contacting their own creative sources in the course of the training. This enlivening process is vital for them in carrying out the work with others.

My perspective also has another source: that of the exploration of my own creativity, primarily in the form of painting. Over the last four or five years, coincident with developing the ISIS-Canada expressive arts therapy training program, I have returned to my own art-work and rediscovered for myself a critical area of liveliness and excitement. In this book, I begin with a painting journal that I kept for a few months while I painted intensively—every day for four to eight hours. In writing about my thoughts and feelings while I was painting and before and after painting sessions, I discovered a sense of a fire within myself that painting uncovered. Not only was the act of painting making me feel hot, but the images that were emerging were themselves burning in different ways. I came to love the images in my paintings, to love the playful way in which I engaged in the painting—putting up the blank sheet of paper, starting some music, and not thinking—and to love the excitement that began to build inside me. I definitely felt an aesthetic response coming from myself, a sense of being moved and, in this way, an inner movement or change occurring.

These diverse perspectives lead me to speak in a variety of voices in this book. In the "Painting Journal," I take a phenomenological attitude. Here I am speaking out of my own experience in a descriptive way. The language is concrete, personal and immediate. Then, I shift into a more theoretical voice which comes from my psychoanalytic training. The language here is more abstract and systematic. It tries to capture the essential structures of the experience of creative aliveness in a conceptual frame. The next section is presented in a clinical voice. Here I take the materials of my clinical experiences and try to interpret their meaning in terms of the creative development of the individuals and the groups with whom I have worked. Again, there is a shift of tone as I deal not so much with concepts but with real people in their relationship to themselves and others. Finally, in the Afterword, I explore some of the ethical implications of expressive arts therapy. Thus, the multiplicity of perspectives in the field of expressive arts therapy is mirrored in the discourse of the different voices which I adopt in this book. It is my hope that these different perspectives will come together in a lively interplay that sparks the reader to find his or her own voice.

This book tries to link a theory about creativity and the self as an inner burning or vitality with the experience of my own fire being ignited and the work that I have done with others to ignite their creative fires. The theorist whom I find to be of most help in contributing to my understanding of the role of creativity in human experience is the British psychoanalyst, D.W. Winnicott, whose work I discuss in Part Two of this book.

I see Winnicott as providing a bridge for me between the work that I have done with children and adults and my own exploration of creative fire both in painting and in training students. I connect quite strongly to this theoretical work because I feel that it has provided support and underpinning for a deeper involvement with the arts and imagination in therapy. Following Winnicott in moving away from the need for certainty, for sense-making and for explanations, and being more willing to be surprised, to follow the image, to *participate* more in the creative process, has been a personal challenge for me. My own character structure sometimes fights against the desire to loosen and flow. I have had to consciously train myself to be quiet and drop down into the patient's world. With children, this has not been difficult because I love to play when I feel relaxed. I try to continue to hold on to the sense-making function but to keep it floating around me while I play and follow the images. Intellectual curiosity is an integral part of me, but, in this kind of therapeutic work, it needs to be kept from taking over. It is useful *afterwards* in terms of understanding what has happened and holding that in mind for the next encounter.

I have come to respect the power of the arts and the creative process. In our culture we tend to keep them separate from everyday life. The place of "real" art is in the museums. Creative individuals are set apart, sometimes deified, sometimes vilified. I see how important it is to affirm that creativity is part of the healthy functioning of all individuals and of societies as well. It makes us more flexible and less rigid, more open and less defended, and provides more comfort with darkness, pain and frustration. Being in formlessness is uncomfortable sometimes because it is possible that destructive and negative aspects of the self may emerge. But as long as creativity is burning, we nourish ourselves.

As expressive arts therapists, I see us as fire tenders. We work in transitional space—with the stuff of play, fantasy, dreams and the arts. We need to provide a holding environment in order to welcome and invite the images which emerge from this work to come in. We need to be responsive to these images once they arrive, not necessarily in terms of providing the correct interpretation which forces us to take a step back and distances us from the material. Rather, we need to stay *engaged* with the images ourselves, to allow them to come inside and to provide a response which fosters their forward movement. There is a danger that intellectualization or contextualization of the images may rob them of their aliveness and power. Too much focus on content may tend to reduce the image to a biographical fact or statement about the condition of the self which is then used for purposes of diagnosis or assessment. Questions about meaning can kill the mystery and the uniqueness of the image, and the fire can be extinguished.

It is my hope that this book stimulates creativity and lights a fire for others. Creativity is part of our individual development. For me, it is also what underlies the concept in the Jewish tradition of *tikkun ha'olam*, the repair of the world. Moving through difficult situations and painful places both personally and globally requires thought and action which is flexible and responsive. Often the arts have played a significant role in the repair of the world by providing a container for pain and suffering. Hopefully, this book will help us to understand how this is possible, and my voice will be one flame that joins with the others in our field to keep the fire alive.

PART ONE

A Painting Journal

During the months of August, September and October of 1993, I kept a journal in which I explored my creative process as a visual artist. I was living on Martha's Vineyard, an island off the coast of Cape Cod in Massachusetts, at that time. My younger son, Jesse, had decided to stay on the Vineyard and attend the high school there. With my older son, Gabriel, leaving home for university as well, it took some adjustment to even consider the idea of our home without the boys. Spending the first few months with Jesse on the island helped to ease the blow of their rather abrupt departure and created a transitional time for Jesse and me.

During this period of transition, I became intensely involved with painting in my new studio. The studio had been completed at the beginning of the summer and, while I did use it quite a bit in July and August, once the summer ended and quiet descended on the island, I felt myself settling down to a routine of painting every day. I had never been able to do this before because work and younger children had consumed all of my time. During this period, my husband, Steve, was on sabbatical from York University in Toronto and was studying in New York.

The experience of large chunks of open time was incredibly powerful for me. I felt that it was a temporary respite and that, if I could allow myself to do it, it would be interesting to structure my time around going inside of myself and exploring my own potential as an artist. My tendency for years had been to go outside, to be with others, to be of service. Sometimes this internal move felt self-indulgent to me. How could I justify this? I felt guilty. Yet when I was able to fully drop in to the artistic space, letting the world go for awhile, I began to feel more refreshed and excited than I had felt in a long time. I kept reminding myself that the time would be over and I would be back to work, being of service to others, soon enough. Yet the ambivalence around giving myself the gift of time and recharging my creativity was strong.

From September 12 to 25 of that year, I showed my paintings in a gallery on the Vineyard. I had spent much of the summer preparing for the show, painting but mostly organizing framing and all the necessary details. It was my first really big show. Although I was joined together with another artist, I had about fifteen paintings there.

The show came about through the support and encouragement of Albert Alcalay, a Boston artist and teacher, who has been a friend of my family's for more than forty years. Albert was my painting teacher when I was young, nine through fifteen years old. He has a home on the Vineyard and has been spending summers there since the mid-1960's. For the past few years, Albert has been involved with my renewed interest in painting and has given me the benefit of his vast knowledge and expertise at several different junctures. In the journal, I refer to him several times. His influence on my work has been significant. Like any master-student relationship, there have been some complexities, and it is interesting to me to read the journal entries and to see the process of evolution of the relationship.

The combination of painting and writing was new for me. At times, I tried to do both at the same time—paint for a few minutes and then immediately describe the action in words. Alternatively, I tried painting for a longer time and then stepping back and reflecting on the process in a less descriptive way. This more reflective stance produced material which went beyond the actual making of the painting. My associations to the images, to the paint itself and to its application, often gave rise to feelings about the world and about my life. Insights began to emerge. By beginning with the tactile and sensory experience of painting, I found that I was better able to think. In this way, I learned that, for me, it is important to experience the ground, the concrete material, and only then to begin to make sense out of it. The meanings are embedded in the material and are intimately connected to it. By engaging in the process of doing and thinking, I discovered what works for me. It seems to me that in the painting journal process, I was actually *enacting* the concept of creativity as primary aliveness which I am trying to develop in this book. To embody the concept is also appropriate in light of the nature of such an idea.

Several themes emerge in the journal. One of the major concerns of the journal seems to be the interplay between structure and freedom. I speak a great deal about *letting go* both in the painting and in my life. The whole way in which I was painting was an attempt to forget about trying, to put the blank paper or the blank canvas up and to clean out my mind. At most, the space was filled with some kind of music, depending on my mood. The music, and the way it either reflected or opposed my mood, was the only starting place. I liked to mix up various paint concoctions. This was often quite random, experimenting with texture and the mixture of materials. I also liked to use my hands to apply the paint. This made the experience even more direct and immediate.

In terms of the content of the paintings, layers always seemed to emerge. I pushed myself at various times to play around with the layers—to soften the defining edges between them and sometimes to try to give them up entirely, allowing the whole painting to be one continuous flow. I often connected this dialogue with layering to the interplay between structure and freedom, or with the related oppostion between merger and separation. I know that separation was on my mind a great deal, particularly in terms of my relationship to my children. Their movement away from the holding container of the family was challenging me to work more on letting go, on opening up and allowing more flow in my relationship to the family. I could see in a concrete way, by means of the visual images, my strong tendency to contain and control embodied in the layers. I also experienced in a tangible way how difficult it was for me to break down the edges between areas of the painting, to let go of the lines. Yet I could feel how enjoyable it was to free the painting up. So this dance between holding on and letting go was active in both painting and life.

Fire became a strong elemental theme in the work. I often experienced myself getting warm from painting. The studio was unheated except for a very small heater which I kept on the painting table right next to my body as I painted.   Despite or perhaps because of the coolness of the space, the images kept reminding me of aspects of fire. I was using a great deal of red and orange during this period. There were central areas of red in the paintings in the early part of the summer, but during this intensive period of work, the red began to grow and to take over the whole painting. The fire that I associated with my paintings was not a fire which consumed its contents and was then extinguished. It was a continuous burning feeling, like the heat that is found near the core of the earth This fire originated in the bottom layer of the painting as a kind of smoldering. As the painting moved upward, the fire underneath began to show itself more and more.   It changed into a more forceful and obvious warmth. I liked using iridescent and interference colors and a great deal of metallic paint in order to get the whole image to shine.

The idea of the *shining forth* of that which is hidden but powerful was important to me. I began to think of the images as connected to myself, to my own way of presenting myself in the world. Without wanting to reduce the image to a mirror of the self, I felt that these images both in the way that they were conceived and created and also in terms of their content were intimately mine. I felt their subtle power in the same way that I experience myself as a subtle person with hidden depths, a person that needs the right environment to allow those deeper places to shine forth.

The fact that I began to love my images, that I felt excited by the creative process and refreshed after long painting sessions, meant to me that I *needed* to paint in the same way that I needed to eat or to be in connection with others. Recognizing that I needed to paint was a significant outcome of this intensive painting time. I could see that the need to paint would be an organizing principle for the next phase of my life. Space was beginning to be cleared by the departure of my children and, despite my intense sadness and longing for more babies, I was moving into this new space and beginning to set up my paints in it. The studio was the literal manifestation of this new space.

By taking the time to explore, without being wedded to the outcome, I had discovered some important things. I had not planned for these things to come up. I did set the stage for something to happen: creating a space for art-making, putting aside significant amounts of unstructured time. Yet setting the stage involved going into the studio without a specific plan or agenda and seeing what would emerge. This journal expresses some of the process of giving up control. I hope that it will be useful to others and provide a model to some who fear going into themselves without knowing where it will lead. After having this experience, I know, in a concrete and bodily way, that art can hold and provide a shape for many disparate and conflicting feelings and thoughts. Painting, for me, is one place where I can feel safe to explore with confidence and trust. I only need to let go and be carried into it.

August 18, 1993

I just finished my last painting in preparation for the show on September 12. I don't know if I like it. There is something wrong and I don't know what it is. Creating the last three paintings has been different. Of course, I've made them on demand

because I needed more work for the show. I've been more critical of these. Also, I've tried to use Albert's suggestions: variation to avoid boredom, paying attention to the angle of the
curves, experimenting with color more, putting blue and gold
together. The results in these new ones look more mannered
to me.

How to take up suggestions and then integrate/incorporate
them into the process without impinging on the spontaneity?
The critic gets activated, ready to leap on me and my products
at the slightest invitation. *Just keep going!!* Are shows still pre-
mature for me? Am I ready for the exposure which is inevitable? People will look and walk away unmoved. Some may
like it, but enough to buy it? A new direction for me. Scary.
We could use the money, no question, but worth? What are
these images worth?

September 10, 1993

Settling down to more of a routine today. Exercise/paint-
ing/writing. Getting the family positioned this year was and
continues to be a massive task. Gabe to McGill. Steve to New
York City. Jesse here with me. Hard for me to find my own
rhythm. I get lost in tasks. I feel afraid of the emptiness and
the quiet of the days here. I need some structure. Take Jesse
to meet the bus in the eary morning and pick him up in the
afternoon about 3:00. Two bookends on the day. In between—
drink tea, eat a bit, exercise, paint, lunch, writing and resting.
Naps are essential because of the early hours. Last night I saw
"Like Water for Chocolate." Rich, sensuous images. The textures of life: fabrics, clothing, knitting, cooking, and the dichotomy between love and passion and rigid authority.

Home is a cocoon, a warm web. Yet it is also a set of
endless tasks like empty holes to fill which cry out "Fix Me!"
Home for me is the stage or the platform for inner creative activity. I have no need to go out of the house or to be with
anyone. How does this work? Steve needs to be out. Being-
with is his favorite, most creative condition. I like going-in most

of the time, cultivating the depth like layers going down. Paolo suggested turning my paintings upside down so the stones fly upward into the sky——LET IT GO, FLY, DISORIENTATION. Going down can be so heavy. Going up is care-less, light. What about all that stuff I wrote about women and creativity—the mountain or the web? But maybe I am still *webbed,* caught in a context despite my aloneness and the comfort of creating alone. What are my contexts now? The "art scene" on Martha's Vineyard. Showing, coming out in public. Selling my work in the marketplace, extending the images out in this way.

The studio is a major context now. It is a beautiful space. The light streams in through all the windows and skylights. It is orderly and calm. The sea-blue floor and the clean white. Big enough to dance in. Music seems to have texture here. The painting process also is a context for me, as I engage in it and allow myself to fall into it.

I began this morning with a smaller white paper, gessoed yesterday. Decided not to draw on the paper first and fill in the shapes as I did in the last set of paintings preparing for the show. Too confining now. No worries about deviating and failure right before the show. No need to keep from taking risks today.

So I go—blue/green thick on the brush and I go—water-flow—same as before, slippery gel leaving openings for stones or something. Enjoying the flow of the paint. Burlap to blot and wipe and leave traces, patterns. Oh—maybe I could use the burlap in collage or something, actually attach it to the paper. Gabe's voice talking about texture and using materials to build up surfaces even more. Burlap might make a good impression of a cliff, a layer. Cover it with paint mixed with extra coarse pumice gel, more build-up, more texture. Albert's voice comes now—put gold next to blue and red near sky. Sky is an intense pink this time. Urge to do more with the burlap—a piece going right across the whole page without stopping. Ripped edges like fences or blades of grass. Bigger paper. Oops! Just realized I was in such a hurry, I forgot the gesso....this is a first. Urge to go on was so strong—hope paper can hold.

Strings falling from burlap find their way below the cliff—maybe like the burning bush. I love working like this with no sense of what is happening. Suspend the outcome and stop judging. PLAY! Playing with the strings. Oh God! I'm playing. It's Friday at 11:00 in the morning and they're working at the agency. The play therapy seminar starts next week and I'm playing!

Struggling lately with taking time off, spending money to just play. Anxiety creeps in. Now I'm lying in bed writing in this book. People are working and historic events are taking place at every moment. Israel signs a pact with the PLO. South Africa will have elections in April. Apartheid will end formally. AMAZING! And I'm just playing. Other people are taking care of things while I take a break. Playing. Let the strings just hang off the burlap. Find a purpose for the cast off strings that takes shape into something interesting. These paintings will dry and I'll make them shine in the next phase. Laying the groundwork and reaping the rewards.

September 13, 1993

ISRAEL/PLO PEACE ACCORD IS SIGNED. Wishing to be in Jerusalem today. Feels momentous.

Paintings of hope. The fire burns from within and sends warmth above. But it is held down. Kept from erupting. The top layer seems calm now. The sky is affected. Not so pretty anymore, a little foreboding but not so much. A green sky? All that black looks good with the red.

Not sure about this other one. [Plate 1] Red sky on red cliff has a good glow. Gold, though, looks too massive and undifferentiated. Need to let it dry and then play with it. I like the rocks with burlap strings around them. Want to work more with rocks and burlap. Next painting—water a little massive. Try irregular purple scribbles around rocks especially. Needs more movement. I like the paintings to be static and in motion at the same time.

Hope is that little bit of movement that you can see. It's
not big and flashy, setting itself up for a big fall. Full of pride
and great expectations. You can kill that kind of hope in a
minute. But the hope I mean is very subtle. Buried under lots
of debris. Waiting to be discovered. Uncovered very carefully
so as not to awake it too quickly. Be gentle with it. Be very
careful. It's glowing. It's turning very slowly......to face.....the
light. It was there for a very long time, lots of garbage kept
getting piled up on top of it. The smelly stuff leaking, leaching
down on top of it, almost putting out the light.

September 14, 1993

Finished two new paintings. Not sure about them but as
explorations they seem fine. Waiting for gesso to dry on new
paper. A time of tension. What will come? Will anything happen?

Begin sweeping. The phone rings (should I have a phone
in here?). It's Amy. Trying to find a time to be together. Next
week we'll meet at the gallery where I have to be with my show
and we'll sit together for awhile. Continue with sweeping. The
studio seems to get dusty so quickly. Little bits and balls of
dust everywhere. Looking up now after so much sweeping,
and there's another puff in a shaft of sunlight. The floor is
scratched too. The radio doesn't hold a station this morning.
Static. Lots of stations fading in and out. Now there's one—
cello and guitar—Bach?

Dealing with the tension of the white page by cleaning.
Once swept, the studio feels lighter, more airy. I love it when
the breeze lifts the air up in here. Wind makes the trees rustle
and whisper. A puff of wind blows hair across my cheek. Static
on the radio. I like the studio swept. A form of readiness.
Preparation to go on to the next one. The end of a painting
always produces a big commotion and mess. To go into it thoroughly, I need to make a mess around me. Things ready to
hand, right on the table. But then the end comes and everything is torn apart. The need for re-ordering is strong.

Taking the paintings down from the wall. Repairing the stapled edges. Setting them out to dry on the floor. Gesso the next piece of paper. And clean. Put things away again. Sweep up the bits of oilstick. Wipe the floor in spots which I've tracked around on the bottoms of my socks. Paying attention. The ritual of cleansing and purifying for the next one. An intuitive process for me which I am only *now* thinking about. Strange. I know that I like ordering and cleaning. Preparing the space. Setting the stage. Setting the table. Beautifying the ground.

Gardening means a lot of preparation. Every year there is a rhythm of readying the earth. After the harvest, turning the earth. Planting the cover crop. Tilling in the crop after the winter. Amending the soil, fertilizing. Every month my body prepares the ground for conception. The cycle is geared for an event for which it must prepare. The painful part of not being able to conceive was the intense energy I put into preparing.

I am a master of preparation. I devote a great deal of time to it. It is a devotion. Also, maintaining is important to me. Sometimes this flips over into the negative: always preparing for it but never *in* it. So much maintaining feels like janitorial duties, being the caretaker. Creativity sometimes gets lost in the details of the movement around the stage. Get onto the stage now. Showing my work feels like that. But the actual doing of the work feels like being in it, on the stage, engaged in the process. Avoiding this is pretty easy but these next few weeks will be my time to try out another way, a way which pays attention, respects my need to prepare but also pushes me to be in the process of painting as much as possible. When will I have an opportunity like this again?

Now on to the blank paper. Wanting to use the burlap more—had a piece that looked like a cliff and I frayed the edge even more. Started with red and then remembered Albert's last words to me as he entered the car on Sunday to leave the island: use red, try all the different reds—cadmium, alizerian crimson. And his voice trailed off speaking of red and then orange, try orange, too. The man of colors. I made peace with him this summer. Stopped fighting his intrusion (meant to write instruction!)

The red is all over the painting. Thinking about white haze on top and black on the bottom with scratching through of red, maybe yellow over the red. Waiting for the paint to dry. Will the burlap stick without glue? Yellow splotches over the red. Used yellow paint to put down some strings near the rocks. Adding more depth or texture or something. Hard to wait until the paint dries. Anxious to get at it. Good thing this is acrylic and not oils. It was hard at first getting used to the fast dry. Now I can't get it to dry fast enough before I want to be at it. So I fool around in the dry places, try the black oil stick over the top. Scratching is good but it looks mysterious when I rub off the black and it leaves a stain. Go over it with irridescent blue and it really starts to shimmer. Now I've added odd little bits of burlap covered with yellow paint. Building up surface again. Love this underneath area. All the dark, strange stuff. Held down. This time there's a straight line across it. No waves. No curves. Will I soften that or just leave it?

September 15, 1993

This one is coming along. Although I'm not sure I like the way the burlap takes the oil stick. It sucks it up. Moulding paste shows off the color more clearly. Drawing with pencil on the burlap might work to get more definition. Feeling confused today. Thinking about work today. Am I missing work or just anxious about money? I love living here but I need a way to make money. To buy art supplies at least! I also miss Toronto in a way. God, what *purpose* I have there. In Toronto, every day is programmed. Working days and sometimes at night. That's why I stepped out—to stay here and feel my own rhythms. I have seemed to structure my days, though. Up at 6:00. Get Jesse off. Eat. Make tea. Go to the studio. Paint. Write. Dance class at 10:00. Home. More painting and writing. Today, pick up Steve, who is visiting, at 3:30, etc. Why not have the structure? I invent my day. Sometimes there are tasks around the house. Next week will be taken up with sitting in the gallery every afternoon.

This painting has a structure like the others but I'm exploring a variation on the theme. New materials. New colors. Slightly different forms. Pushing myself to explore. The tendency for me is to stay in the same place. Stay home. Stay safe. How seldom do I just wander? Toronto life is so busy, so programmed, but regular income gives comfort. Lately I have been feeling anxious and uncomfortable. Money going out and *none* coming in, no paintings have sold yet. Steve says not to worry. We're borrowing money now and we'll pay it back. A *temporary* situation, yes, yes, remember. Soon enough I'll be walking up the city streets to my office and this time will be over. Relax, open to the air, the peace, the quiet, the time to wander and to create. Explore. Let go. Wander.

September 20, 1993

Monday. Steve left yesterday to go back to New York. In confusion and with a lot of sadness. We had a close time together so the separation feels poignant. Staying centered while he struggles....I need to give encouragement, to have empathy. Love for him rising up and expressing itself lately more and more. The loss of him feels sad although a relief as usual in some respects. I can get back to myself when he's gone. Sometimes he takes up all the space. I spend a lot of my time attending to him emotionally and physically, psychically. Not *necessary* but it's what happens.

It seems like years since I was in here last but it's only been five days. The weather is turning so it's cooler in here than before. Feels different, less comfortable. A challenge to keep going here, continue painting and exploring. Time is a bit more limited, sitting now at the gallery every afternoon. Very quiet there. Will people come this week? It has to be clear that I paint now because I want to do it. Yet there is a need for recognition in it. Putting the work out there in the world is a big step but not without its rewards. Does it matter that people appreciate my work and yet don't actually buy it? I have been getting pretty tense lately when I anticipate that someone will buy and then they don't. I don't really know how to sell my work. But, at this point, selling is not the focus of the effort behind doing it. I know that every artist struggles with this. I am very glad that I don't have to sell my work to eat. The response to my work has been very good. This is the reward for now. Be content. Remember—back to the office soon enough!

Returning to the last image—the experiment with burlap and collage. The pieces look flat to me today. Begin with moulding paste to build up the surfaces of the rocks. Cover the red cliffs with gold paint and then the green fringe of grass. The overall effect still seems flat. We'll see what happens when the moulding paste dries.

Gessoed a big piece of paper. Feeling like letting go more today. I remember a big piece that I did several summers ago, Still one of my favorites. The feeling of freedom from just letting the brush go free and lead my hand. Can you *plan* for that to happen again? Is any plan contrary to the spirit of freedom? Back to the idea of structure and its relation to expression. It makes me think about teaching: my challenge is to *let go* more, to explore and to see what happens with that. Let the students do more of the work, the questioning and the finding out. I want to experiment with making a strategic input so that students can then truly learn by experience. But what is the strategic input or the role of the teacher? A provocation? Helping to brainstorm ideas and then letting them carry out the ideas? Leading them to the resources? Myself as a resource: I'm here but you have to formulate the question. What do *you* need me for? Being-with rather than doing-for. An attentiveness to the process of the other. Not to have to *be* the other and get them to do it my way. I can be so controlling both with my children and with my students.

New painting. Much more energy. Exciting to let go with the red, to really be big and free. Another in the Layering Series format but yet different. Finished up last painting while the red of the new one drying. It's OK but a little placid—not enough movement for me. New painting. Experiment with leaving brown stones as they are, without embellishing or going over them. A bit of green? More natural colors. Time to go. Too bad. I'm warm now and into it......

September 21, 1993

Wood preparations this morning in anticipation of rain predicted this afternoon. Collecting, stacking, storing. I definitely have the "ant mentality." Plan ahead. Anticipate. Be ready for what is expected. How about the unexpected? Only be poised and flexible to receive it. That's all one can do. Looks like the house might be rented for November 1. I feel relieved and a bit lighter at the thought of being able to cover the mortgage now. Never had to worry about these things before— maybe a good dose of reality for Steve and I at this point. Most people worry about money all the time.

Working on the red painting now, using and exploring various shades of red (Albert's voice trails off—he is also present here with me at the gallery, a photograph of his face amongst other artists on the Vineyard. His face is in repose, looking away and down, eyes somewhat troubled). Hard to stay with the painting process without digressing too much. Also hard to write about this morning from afar, sitting here at the gallery, not right in front of the painting itself. What do I remember now from the activity of the morning?

Finishing the black area, scratching out the red. Blue on the bottom looks too smooth and placid. Green squiggles liven it up quite a bit. Back to the red, keeping it as red but varying the tones—oranges, brighter reds, flourescent colors make it burn at the edges. Up to the sky—yellow tempered or dulled by turquoise then irridescent and interference gold over the top. Build up of paint areas over with gold. Starting to shine.

September 22, 1993

Keith Jarrett. Vienna Concert, 1992. Pulsing, free-ranging improvisation with Keith grunting and breathing hard and heavy, singing. Let it go, let it go. Rumbling left hand, ranging all over the keyboard with the right. Stopping. Starting. Gasp. Breathe. The painting unfolds. Now I'm dwelling in the black area—interference gold to shroud the rocks at first. Makes them ghost-like and mysterious. Apply the paint with my finger. Rough surface smooths the prints off my fingertip and leaves it feeling a bit raw.

Now Keith's back to a tune with the rolling rhythm behind. Groaning...the beauty of it. It rolls up and down. Southern slave melody. Gospel. Romantic. Beautiful but painful. Pause to emphasize the tune. Taking time to feel the simplicity of the tune and its majesty at the same time. Sad. Like an ending. Parting. Lovers parting. Holding on until the last minute. Waving goodbye as the boat pulls away. Long journey ahead into the unknown. A sad ending but resigned and resolved in some ways.

Side Two. Beginning as an exploration. Wandering. Wondering. Eastern quality. Searching. Left hand pushing the right hand to go on. Middle Eastern feel. Insistent. Building in intensity. I *want*. Dissolves. Sweep it clean. Start again. A faint drum behind ? Banging but soft. Now back into the rolling and building again. It's pretty dark. Mystery. Like where I'm painting and exploring now. Down under in the dark space. Trying to illuminate the dark, to find the glowing fire down there. There is gold in the dark place. Toying with another simple melody only now with the right hand, without the drive of the left. But Keith can't help it. He starts driving it again. A faint drum to emphasize. Then he quiets it down totally and lets it escape through one or two notes. Until it totally fades away and the crowd explodes in applause at the end.

On the album liner, Keith says: "I have courted the fire for a very long time, and many sparks have flown in the past, but the music on this recording speaks, finally, the language of the flame itself." Yes, Keith! I'm with you. But you also smolder like glowing embers. Like the red places in my paintings that burn in places, simmer in others and melt away. Or like the dark underneath layers which contain burning places. Glow on, Keith!

I finished the red painting today. I really like this one. It has more intensity. For me, it glows. Did Keith help? I didn't know he was working on fire in that piece. There must be a connection.

Now I put my last two large ones side by side. It feels as though in these two the firey force has escaped and pushed the curtain aside. The most recent one is more open and vulnerable. The shape floating in the red is very soft inside after all. The forms in black lie soft and contained. After the eruption, things are more settled. Rocking, bobbing, very pleasing.

September 23, 1993

Jesse is sixteen today. Time. Time. Time. Mixing up the brightest red I can find. Put on the Vienna Concert again. Warming up. Feel the creaminess of the paint. Soft. Warm. Edible. Paint begins to go on. This time red fills up the whole space except for the holes/rocks/openings. How smooth and easy it is, like the music. Slow and melodic now. A sadness there.

I'm thinking about myself at the center of the family now. We're all apart this year. Jesse is moving out even as he is in with me for this period of transition. Soon he'll live away from me. Let go. Keith is beginning to let go now. The rumble and the beat come in. Finding my own way. Having another baby was so strong for me. But if I tell the truth about it or one truth, anyway, it was about *holding on*

> to family, to the whole
> to youth
> to a connection to child-things
> to communities of women caring for children

to pleasure
to body

The daughter. This missing daughter who could be my friend and companion. But who can predict how that turns out? I know it's not always so wonderful between mothers and daughters. But I was willing to try it. It would have been an adventure. The baby was for holding on just a little longer. I know that she would go too someday. Now these babies that I have are going. Steve, too, in his way wants to go and to stay at the same time. Me at the hub of it. Letting go now. Focusing in for this period. Feels freeing. If there were another child, would I be in this studio now, exploring so much? Who knows? Would there have been the other things in my life—social work training, clowning, Hincks, ISIS? Maybe I could have done it all as usual. Music picking up now. Keith is rolling all over the keyboard. I'm putting on moulding paste and then pumice. Things are starting to open here. Hands all over—scratching, rolling, patting. Looks wilder now. Will I tame it? Watch that. Let it go.

September 24, 1993

No painting today. People are sleeping in the studio. A Russian man and his Polish girlfriend—Avi and Marta. He speaks English, she speaks none. They arrived on the boat last night, looking for the Jewish community for Yom Kippur services. Steve invited them to our house. Wanderers who depend on the kindness of others. How long has it been since we have encountered people like this? An element of mistrust sets in. Who are they? What do they really want? An attempt to keep some distance. A care-ful boundary so they don't move in here and take over the space. One night is enough. Fed and housed, I drop them at the beach. Probably they'll show up here later to see the gallery and keep the connection going.

We want to be open and generous to strangers. Our hearts go out to the wayfarers, the pilgrims. Avi said, "Ha-Shem will take care of things," last night as he left the boat. But there is a sense of privacy and limits, appropriateness. How have we learned this? In Judaism, we are taught to open our doors, to feed strangers—"for you were once strangers..." Where are the models for this? Did my parents ever do this directly? Steve's? They gave to charity but it was from a distance. These are bold people, Avi and Marta; they are not helpless but they depend upon the goodwill of others. They try to give back what is possible—they offer to cook us a meal (our ingredients, of course!). He offered to make a "very special tea" for us and took all of our teas, mixing them with honey. I said I'd thought he had brought a special Russian tea. I did expect for him to give more in return. He was critical of some of the spiritual communities that he had visited recently—Kripalu/Guru Dev tries too hard to appeal to Westerners, too watered down and Omega is too tense and controlled. They leave "gifts" for us: a crystal, a small agate stone, an unidentifiable metal object for Jesse. Did we live up to their expectations or did we, too, fall short?

Homelessness is different from this. Do homeless people have choices? These people work when they want to and live from other people. They are responsible for themselves. What if you decide not to take them in? Should you feel guilty because you're not being generous enough? Maybe if they were homeless and victims of forces beyond their control....and then?

September 28, 1993

Trying to hold back from cleaning up the studio this morning. Stay with the process and not get distracted. I feel the pull of all the things that need to be done before I go back in a month—four weeks left. In some ways, it feels like a relief to be going back—to the certainty of my schedule, to the insertion into a world of work and purpose, to a regular income (although I should be making more money). In other ways I am sad about leaving—this beautiful space, Jesse, my friends, my *time*. I have to decide what to do in the remaining time. The next month will be busy with trips and visitors. There won't be enough time for everything so prioritizing is essential:

1. painting and writing
2. preparing for teaching when I return
3. household tasks—getting ready for winter

It seems that continuing to paint is really essential. When will I ever get this opportunity again? I keep feeling this. So everyday, I need to make a commitment to be in the studio for the morning. Then I can have the afternoon free for preparation for teaching and the household tasks. This sorting is essential for me to do right now, otherwise I can feel myself getting overwhelmed by how much there is to do and how little time is left.

Looking back at what I wrote on the 23rd. I was experiencing freedom which for me was/is not easy. It was exciting to paint and experience the convergence with the music, the music penetrating my experience of painting. The application of the paint, the scratching, the mushing with my hands. Very direct and immediate. No brushes to mediate, no technique to get in the way. Of course, the other side is that technique can open things up as well. Now I'm looking at the painting as the second stage takes shape—the adornment stage. The wildness is getting tamed somewhat. My task for today might be to return some of the wildness to the painting. Somehow, though, I would rather not try to do anything at this point. Let's just see what happens next.

Yes. I'm moving it now. Decided to change the whole sky thing. Looking less like a landscape now and more underground, below, and afire. In the core is an exciting coolness now.

September 29, 1993

Finishing up. I love this painting. It has more life and energy. The top layer doesn't press down. It seems to rise up and shine through with possibilities. The large rock seems so tranquil—maybe it needs some red inside of it. How can something be so contained in the midst of such a fiery and alive place? It *floats* on fire but is not touched.

The lights are off but this painting shines. I like the way I've torn up or scratched out the edges of the layers so these areas are more permeable, less defined, and they press down less severely. Maybe the task for the next few paintings is to make the layers less and less obviously discrete. This might be good to explore for awhile.

October 4, 1993

Back from New York last night. Hard to get started this morning. It's a bit chilly and the deer seem to have eaten up the garden. Forgot to pick up the mail. Sometimes when I'm here I forget about the outside world.

New York was an assault on the senses—noise, smells in the subway, a riot of color, chaos and the *suffering*. At times it was unbearable. A small black woman curled in fetal position, barefoot and dazed, shaking. Lying on the corner of 52nd and 6th, beside the newspaper boxes and the trash cans. On the bare pavement. I can't get the image of her out of my mind. Feeling helpless to help. She wasn't really asking for help—too weighted down by her inner experience.   It's too big and if you get involved, what happens then? All a bunch of total rationalizations. But I did think about what I would do, where I would take her. It was obviously drugs, possibly crack. I bet she has babies somewhere. But I passed her by just like everyone else did.

Saw a lot of paintings in New York. Jackson Pollacks at MOMA: some which are pure explosion and others I had never seen which have patterning and some structure. Komar and Melamid: in a series of technically perfect paintings, Stalin commits suicide in a seedy motel somewhere in America.   Polish painter living in Paris and painting on cardboard. DeKooning and Dubuffet: disappointing because so decorative and no edge.

Three new ones on the go today. I can feel the excitement of having looked at paintings this weekend. This pushes me to keep exploring with texture. Even did one on cardboard in purple instead of red. I'm conscious now of wanting to break down the distinctions between layers. On the purple one—a new way of playing with the matte knife which leaves different tracks from the brush action. The brush traces look like leaves, wrinkles in skin or scars from burns. The matte knife leaves tracks like stratification in rock ledges. Feel sad that I have to leave these now to dry.

October 5, 1993

Restless night, worrying about renting this house as all leads have dried up. Can we manage? I *hate* worrying about money!! It's some kind of curse which I'm sure affects most people. This morning I've put ads in the papers and listed it with an agent. Will put signs all around and then hope.... Taking action actually makes me feel much better. Steve is on his way home. I feel somehow rushed to get things done today, as if when he arrives, I won't be able to do anything anymore.

Three paintings at the same time. The cardboard is pleasing. A strong surface that holds the texture. A bigger piece would be exciting—to build up and scratch off without worrying about taking off the surface of the material. Instead of taking off, I wanted to say destroy—but I didn't. I don't like to destroy things. I like to flirt with destruction from a safe place. Building up and scratching off to reveal what lies underneath. But not building up, destroying, and re-construction. You work with what you have and get deeper, richer with it.

Another exploration has been: being conscious again of breaking down distinctions between areas on the page. So layers begin to blend and intermingle, losing their separateness. The smallest one begins with the boundary firmly in place. It's obvious, and I've even emphasized it through texture, form, and color. It has clarity and resolve. Two substances encounter each other and remain unchanged. The next one lets go—into the fire. [Plate 2] There is a subtle boundary here but the elements are made of the same materials. It's all fire and yet the stones are charred but not consumed. Above the line, the energy travels upward, an eruption but not an explosion. In the third one, the boundaries are back again—this time a relationship between three areas. Blue and green interpenetrate but orange is completely separate. Not sure how I like green against orange, not fond of this combination but I'll leave it for now. Finish it tomorrow.

October 6, 1993

One week until I leave for California and then only five days left after that. I feel it beginning to slip away, my precious time and space here. Feeling some pressure to keep producing and putting out. Surely I could weave some of this work into my life away from here. Balance, balance, it's all about balance..

New paintings are very orange. Still unsure about green against orange but I'm leaving it. It feels fine to put something out in the world that is a question, unresolved. Now I am facing a small canvas and a fairly large piece of paper. Both are all white. I'm going to specify their stages in turn.

Small canvas. Stage One. Applied absorbent ground and built up the texture. White surfaces make me feel like cleaning. The aftermath of finishing a painting. Moving to the ritual of starting new which is a purification.

Large paper. Stage One. Gesso to strengthen it. A beautiful piece of paper. Somehow, luckily, I have not felt intimidated by the cost of this piece of paper. Looks like this one said $15.00. Wow! Stage Two. Mixing bright yellow and gel to get a shine from underneath, maybe a light from underneath. Yellow changes to orange and then to red as we move down. Textures shift from layer to layer. Stage Three. Moulding paste glopped on with my hands, impression of stones.

Small canvas. Stage Two. All red, but the texture from the absorbent ground defines certain areas. See what absorbent ground does to change texture and color. As it dries it looks

different: takes the shine off the paint in certain areas. Stage
Three. Moulding paste glopped on over the open spaces. Stage
Four. Moulding paste is dry. Now to the adornment with oil
sticks. Begin with gold but it looks dead over the red. Move
to violet and then green. Just not right. Rub it all out. Orange—Yes—top area (cliffs?) begins to come alive. Tried dark
green-blue on bottom (water?)—too dark and muddy. Wiping
it off leaves stains. Irridescent purple starting to shine. Wipe
this off and red comes through from underneath—odd, red sea.
Texture really starting to come through. Wiping off the orange
now too—blurring layers, blurring distinctions. Silver on the
top (sky?) Wipe it off. Try irridescent pink. Strong definition
now. Wipe with a tissue. Leaves a nice shine. Not sure about
blue below and pink above. Try irridescent purple below. Better. Scraping with the knife reveals more red, more texture.
Working on the blobs (rocks?). Sensing some boredom coming up in me. Am I getting tired of these now? Trying to come
up with new ideas—the trying creates the boredom. Now with
flourescent red—a fire is starting from one of the deep places.
Another layer is forming and it's fire. It's connecting now to
the orange layer—some integration that comes up from a deep
place, way within. Creates flames on the edge. A burning sea
but, again, the contents are not consumed. Going over it to
make it more subtle now. Didn't like the bright gold on the
big rock. Now it looks more a part of the cliff, emerging out
of it rather than stuck on. Finished.

I go back and forth between going in and coming out. Sub-
tlety and fire. The smoldering embers and the full flame.

October 8, 1993

Large paper. Stage Four. The adornment with oil sticks.
Try a number of colors to stain the orange. Nothing works until the maroon. Then scratching reveals the orange from underneath. A band emerges across the top next to the sky.
Creamier red and then scrape it away with the knife. Scraping
harder and harder. More fire is coming up from underneath.

Put bright orange over top layer to brighten it even more. Gray over yellow sky and wipe it away. Keep wiping and yellow starts to warm the gray. Black over red. Very difficult. The rough surface hurts my fingers. Gold paint over the top is creamy, soothing but I'm not sure about the effect. Love the shiny turquoise at the very bottom. Gold and turquoise look good together. Gold looking too massive, scraping reveals black and red underneath. This is much more interesting.

October 12, 1993

Now that the gold has dried, going over it with orange brightens it which looks better today. Now over the blue with violet. This looks better with orange above but maybe needs scraping. Yes. This is the last big painting before leaving, I'm sure. It follows one that I did two years ago called "Burning Through" which was dark and brooding. This new one looks as if the weather has cleared and the whole world is aglow, just as I feel these days of living on the Vineyard: warmth, love, friendship, relaxation, and opening up. How sad to be leaving this place and leaving my child here. How can I be doing this? Will it be OK for him? Is finishing a painting like leaving a child, especially a child who is still young and only beginning to form? But maybe his life is his canvas to make the right revisions and amendments. How much should I be doing of this forming process anyway? I know that I tend to get too involved and to take charge. It is a bit like making the painting, putting it out there and letting other people have it, have their reactions, appropriate in their own way.

Again I'm back to the idea of letting go. Now Jesse seems ready and poised to slide out. I need to let him slide out. He's chosen to stay here on the Vineyard. He's made his friend-ships; he seems so much happier; he's launching himself now. The Vineyard will hold him—the safe space of life here in a caring community. I feel confident that he'll be OK. That ena-bles me to let go now. I need to feel safe too.

I can't stop painting yet. This would be to fully admit the end of this time and space into my self. I'm not ready yet to go back. I'm not sure I'll ever be ready because, in the back of my mind, is the sense that we'll return here soon. Of course, I know when we are back in Toronto, life will be so busy and we'll feel compelled to say: how can we leave all this? But maybe there's a way somehow to come back here to live and to travel to Toronto regularly, we'll see.

Gessoed two tiny pieces of cardboard. Maybe a dyptich as I look at them together. Need to clean and purify the studio now before I begin to paint them.

Orange undercoating. Each has a different textural arrangement but they're related. Let them dry now.

October 26, 1993

Tuesday morning. Back from California. This feels like the last day in the studio. Too much to do to get ready to leave on Saturday. Packing. Errands. Bills to pay. Arrangements. The stuff of life. Toronto. Toronto. Toronto calling. Time to come back. Gotta go.

Looking around the studio. Much happened in here—parties, gatherings, meetings, rehearsals, and lots of painting. Still it looks fresh from all that. As if it could hold a great deal more before getting weary. Not a depressing space. White and wide open. It can contain mess. Question: how much mess will be possible in here? Will I allow it? With groups, practicing letting go will be challenging.

I can feel myself avoiding feelings now. Leaving is so sad but I'm not feeling it now. Last night I let the sadness come about leaving Jesse—listening to him play the piano made me cry. We talked with him. I cross my fingers that he's absorbed something from us and that it will carry him.

In the paintings today there is an easy, loving but firm touch. Texture holds the glow and carries it. When they were just orange, these two little ones seemed connected. Now with the color over the top, they've differentiated. I love their textures and the glow of gold. Texture provides a sense of activity and movement which flows and is not static. I see a big black crow in the tree outside the door. It makes the branch bob up and down. It looks around quietly. Alert. Studious. Looking for something. Or is it just experiencing? It flies off suddenly and another appears. Then they are both gone.

Goodbye Studio. I love you. I'll dream about you. I'm keeping you alive inside of me. I'll take you with me. Your whiteness, blueness. The light, air, and space. In a way, you and all your potential are my new child. I will nurture you and treasure you. Thanks.

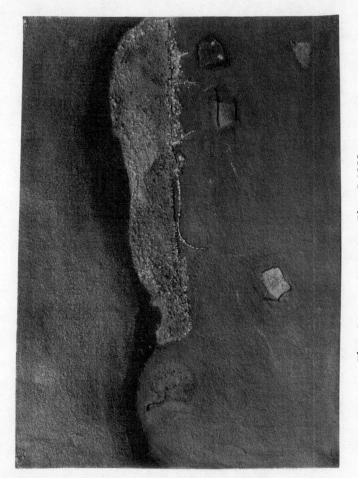

Plate 1   "Morning Glow," 1993

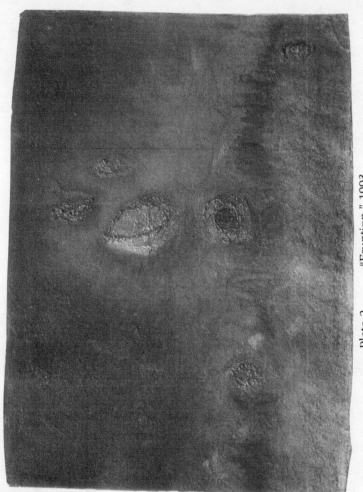

Plate 2   "Eruption," 1993

Homo faber is the man of surfaces, his mind is fixed on a few familiar objects, on a few crude geometric forms. For him, the sphere has no center, it is simply the objective counterpart of the rounding gesture he makes with his cupped hands. On the other hand the *dreaming man* seated before his fireplace is the man concerned with inner depths, a man in the process of development. Or perhaps it would be better to say that fire gives to the man concerned with inner depths the lesson of an inner essence which is in the process of development: the flame comes forth from the heart of the burning branches.

Gaston Bachelard, *The Psychoanalysis of Fire*

PART TWO

Tending the Fire: Towards a
Theory of Creativity in Therapy

Introduction

In this part of the book, I am interested in understanding the work that we do as artists and as therapists and in finding or developing an appropriate theoretical context for this work. Keeping the painting journal enabled me to begin this reflection from my own experience of the creative process and what that means for me in a more personal sense. Now I would like to move from my own experience, using it as a base, toward a reflection on creativity from a wider, more inclusive perspective. Much of our work in the expressive and creative arts therapies is practical and hands-on; and much of the literature, particularly in the journals, is an attempt to document and to describe this work in concrete terms to others. As arts therapists, conceptualizing may not come naturally to us. Some of us may actually be hostile to abstractions. Some of us may ask: why do we need to theorize since this kind of activity just detaches us from experience and we strive so much to be connected to our experience?

My sense is that we have undervalued the role of concepts in our profession and that our capacity to connect and to communicate with other professionals and with those who do not know of our work has suffered accordingly. We put so much emphasis upon being and doing but rarely do we try to understand and to reflect upon our whole project in terms of bringing together the discipline of the arts with the work of change. To truly integrate our doing as artists and therapists with the important and essential activity of reflection is a challenge for us. If we can embrace theorizing as another form of expression and befriend it, our work will certainly go deeper and become more grounded. Finding new ways to think about and to make sense of the work may even provide a new sense of excitement for ourselves and for the work itself.

This book is about the process of creativity as a vitalizing and revitalizing force in our experience. The sustaining theme of the book connects this aliveness and vitality to an internal experience of fire, one which I discovered for myself in the process of exploring creatively and which is documented in the journal. I am using the metaphor of fire to understand, in a theoretical sense, the importance of creativity in firing up the self and the connection between the maintenance of the fire of creativity and the maintenance of aliveness in the self. I want to understand the way in which creativity emerges from the earliest experiences of the infant and the mother and is sustained or not sustained throughout our lives. Like a fire, imagination and creativity must first be built up and then ignited. I will show in this part of the book how creativity emerges and how the symbolic dimension of experience is built up from the very beginnings of human life. Once creativity is formed, it must also be attended to and nurtured. What happens if it goes blazing out of control, or if it dies out completely? I will try to understand the ways in which the aliveness and the vitality of the self, understood as *primary creativity*, is either sustained or diminished by this process of *tending the fire*.

I see an essential function of the therapy process as attending to and a tending of the sense of aliveness in the self. This aliveness does not necessarily presume joy or ecstasy. It encompasses the whole of our felt or lived experience: joy and pain, ecstasy and despair. The activity of tending can often be done in the context of relationships. At times, it also can be done alone. When we stay in relationship and pay attention to our context, we become aware of the whole range of human feeling. When we stay by ourselves but in connection to our aliveness, we become self-reflective and more self-aware. Tending to the self brings us into connection with our creativity.

The artistic process performs the essential function of providing a form or shape for creative expression. The use of the arts in therapy, then, has the potential to unite the attention to the primary aliveness of the self with the recognition of the self in the form of the work of art. The work of art becomes the embodiment of the alive self because its form has been generated from creative, alive activity. The work of art also stands on its own and can enliven and stimulate others as they witness the work and get drawn into it, provoked or moved by it.

Building the Fire: Phantasy and the Formation of the Self

Before the fire can be lit, it must be built. How do we come to be creative, to be able to represent our experience in symbolic and artistic forms? To understand the emergence of these capacities for us as human beings, we will turn to the work that has been done in psychoanalytic theory on the role of creativity in the formation of the self. I have been interested for some time in the way that creativity and self-formation are inextricably linked for certain psychoanalytic thinkers, particularly Melanie Klein and D. W. Winnicott. I have found their ideas to be stimulating and to have given me guidance in the work that I have done with children over the years. It is to their work that I turn in attempting to understand the relationship between the arts and therapy. Yet in order to understand the work of these two important thinkers, it is necessary to return to their point of origin, to Freud. Both Klein and then Winnicott drew their ideas from the work of Freud, especially his later work where he tried to understand the relationship between phantasy and reality in terms of the role of the symbol as bridge between the two worlds. While it is not possible here to discuss Freud's entire project, I will highlight certain material which focuses on the theme of this book, namely the source of our creative life and the capacity which we have to represent our experience imaginatively.

In the essay, *Beyond the Pleasure Principle* (1920), Freud attempts to revise his conception of the original pleasure-pain model of mental functioning, according to which human beings naturally seek pleasure and attempt to avoid pain. He found that this way of conceiving mental life could not account for certain instances whose general pattern seemed to be the repetition of painful experiences, such as, traumatic neurosis, certain children's games, and the compulsion to repeat characteristic of patients whom he saw in therapy. These examples go beyond the explanatory powers of the pleasure principle. Their source can be derived from a single root: the attempt to restore mastery over a situation in which the ego has been wounded or, more precisely, where primary narcissism or self-regard has been dealt a blow. This restoration of the self is in the interests of self-preservation, yet it is accomplished in all three instances by a regressive movement away from reality towards phantasy. This movement takes place also in dreams, play and free association in therapy. In the traumatic neuroses, the individual repeatedly dreams about the original traumatic event where he was powerless to act because he was subject to forces outside of himself. By repeating the experience of being passive, he becomes active and therefore restores in the act of dreaming, through images, the lost sense of his own power.

In this essay, Freud relates a famous occasion where he observed a child of a year and a half, whose mother had gone away, play a repetitive game with a wooden reel. It is in this game where the child makes an object appear and disappear repeatedly that Freud locates a striking example of symbolic restoration. The child would throw the reel over the side of his crib and pull it back up again by the string attached to it. Each time the child threw it away, he would say "o-o-o-o-o" which sounded like *"fort"* (gone) and each time he pulled it back up, he would say *"da"* (there) in a joyful manner. Freud maintained that this game is part of a normal developmental process whereby the weak ego of infancy attempts to strengthen its hold on reality. The child has experienced the pain of separation from the mother, a process in which he felt himself to be acted upon. The game is a re-creation of this situation in phantasy but an overcoming of the painful feelings at the same time. This time it is the child itself that sends the parent away and brings her back. Thus, the child can be active in the situation and restore narcissistic self-regard. This move away from reality into phantasy play, for Freud, has the ultimate purpose of bringing the individual closer to the mastery of reality and serves as an example of the progressive function of regression.

The discussion of the role of play and repetition in the formation of the ego and its relation to reality leads Freud to speculate about the nature of instinctual life as a whole. The compulsion to repeat is an instinct (like the fundamental drive of sexuality): the drive of the organism to return to a state of complete non-being (inertia) out of which becoming can arise. Freud calls this the death instinct and sees it as the desire for the condition of primary narcissism, of a complete union with the other once again. In *Beyond the Pleasure Principle,* Freud postulates the existence of the death instinct as the primary force of organic life in general. Its power is offset by the life instincts which direct us toward objects for the sake of self-preservation. Thus, the basic tension of organic existence is between the regressive force of the death instincts and the progressive force of the life instincts. As Freud points out by means of this *fort-da* game, the phantasized form (as an image of the original experience) serves the purpose of strengthening the ego's mastery over the external world. Thus, the death instinct ultimately pulls backward in order to lead forward. For Freud, what is implied here is a new conception of the function of phantasy. Instead of being considered as an aspect of our experience which we must put aside and go beyond, phantasy is seen as essential in aiding us to get a better grasp on reality. The *fort-da* game is an example of a normal developmental process. The fact that this process is common to all individuals makes it central to an exploration of the origins of symbolic activity.

Much of the work of the British object-relations psychoanalyst, Melanie Klein, came out of this later thinking of Freud's where he tried to understand the role of phantasy and symbol-making activity in the constitution of the self. I have found Klein's work to be extremely important in its consideration of the fundamental basis of our earliest experience in symbolic activity. Her work is exciting because it pushes thought into new and fertile areas, lending insight to the question of where the fire of creativity originates in human experience. Klein's writing itself has an imaginal quality to it. She is not afraid to be daring and to strike out into new territory for the sake of advancing our understanding. Her work of imagining herself inside of the infant is itself a creative act.

One difference between Klein and Freud which is important from the outset is the fact that, although she worked with adults as well, Klein developed her theoretical framework primarily out of her work with children. While the emphasis in psychoanalysis had been on the analysis of childhood experience, it was usually seen retrospectively, that is, from the vantage point of adulthood. Since Klein thought the child's phantasies were crucial in terms of understanding unconscious conflicts, she was able to come to her own conclusions about these conflicts on the basis of contact with very young children in the analytic situation.

At first Klein was hesitant about seeing very young children in analysis. It was widely accepted at the time that only latency-aged children were suitable for analysis. However, through her own experimentation, Klein discovered that even two or three year-olds could have insight into the workings of their minds and could understand interpretations if they were couched in the child's own language. Klein considered interpretations to have the power to reach down into the deepest layer of the unconscious.

As Hannah Segal notes, Klein took "... her cue from Freud's (1920) observations of the child's play with the reel" (Segal, 1973, p. 2). The child's phantasy and play activities provided a source of communication much like free association in adult analyses.

The psychoanalytic play technique, which Klein came to call her method, gave her insight into "...early development, into unconscious processes, and into the nature of interpretations by which the unconscious can be approached..." (Klein, 1975 B, p. 122). In terms of the question of interpretation, Klein was very clear on the connection between Freudian dream interpretation and the interpretation of symbolic communication through play. Play gives us access to the unconscious for Klein in the same way that dreams are the "royal road" to the unconscious for Freud. Play, like the dream, involves an archaic mode of expression because it is bound up with the child's phantasies, wishes and earliest experiences. Like the elements of the dream, the elements of play have many different meanings, and "...we can only infer and interpret their meaning when we consider their wider connections and the whole analytic situation in which they are set" (Klein, 1975 B, p. 8).

Child analysis differs from adult analysis for Klein because the child's unconscious is more accessible to the analyst. She states that the connections between conscious and unconscious are closer in young children than adults, and infantile repressions are less powerful. Through play, the child "acts out" what cannot be expressed in words. In a paper tracing the development of the psychoanalytic play technique, Klein notes that she became more interested in the notion of the symbolic language of play as it related to each child's particular configuration of anxieties and conflicts. Pursuing this line of thought, she was led to certain theoretical insights about the connection of play, the process of symbol formation, and the developmental process:

> Play analysis had shown that symbolism enabled the child to transfer not only interests, but also phantasies, anxieties, and guilt to objects other than people. Thus a great deal of relief is experienced in play, and this is one of the factors that makes it so essential for the child (Klein, 1975 B, p. 138).

Thus it is not only the interpretation of unconscious conflicts but the actual playing itself, as a symbolic act, which provides relief. For the child, being able to play and to express itself symbolically is a crucial part of the developmental process. In fact, Klein found that being inhibited in "... the capacity to form and use symbols, and so to develop phantasy life, is a sign of serious disturbance" (Klein, 1975 B, p. 138). She found this inability to symbolize in the condition of schizophrenia, for example.

For Klein, phantasy forms the basis of psychic life from the beginning. Without dwelling in too much detail on Klein's specific ideas about psychological structure, it is important to note some of the basic features. Klein was primarily interested in the experiences of very early infancy, the first six months of life, which, in her view, formed the basis of all future development. In her work with children, Klein felt that she was able to detect the presence of very early developmental conflicts even though these children were older and presumably had gone beyond these issues. She found the presence of pre-oedipal, pre-genital issues and primitive defences such as splitting or projection used to deal with the anxiety over these primitive conflicts. She also found that very young children were struggling with issues that had always been attributed to later developmental junctures: i.e., children as young as two and a half years displaying phantasies and anxieties about threatening parental images and excessively punishing and savage super-egos.

In order to try to explain these observations, Klein postulated the existence of an ego from the very beginning of post-natal existence; relationships with others (objects) begin at birth, being fundamentally connected to the feeding situation. This earliest ego is of course quite rudimentary; and although it lacks coherence, it performs the function of defending against the primordial anxiety generated by the death instinct. The ego, then, must deal with the struggle between the life and death instincts. In this sense Klein seems to solidify Freud's later theory of the duality of the instincts by taking the ego much further back in development. The ego, as representative of the life instinct, must preserve itself against the death instinct as primordial anxiety. It does so by the process of splitting.

Splitting occurs in the very first experience of the infant and its world. Klein's view of the infant's earliest experience is one of extreme helplessness and dependency. This condition generates a life and death struggle where the main object of attachment is the breast. For the infant, the breast holds all goodness; when it does not appear, it is experienced as bad and punishing. By splitting the breast into good and bad, the infant begins to bring inside (introject) the good aspects of the breast. Repeated experiences of gratification at the breast give rise to the experience of enjoyment and gratitude, a trust in the goodness of the breast and in one's own goodness at the same time. The feeling of being deprived either due to an unhappy feeding situation or the infant's own excessive store of destructive impulses can lead to excessive craving and a greedy, envious attitude toward the breast.

What is interesting for our purposes here is the importance that Klein places upon the role of phantasy/imagination from the very beginning of life: the good and bad breast are phantasies which are generated in order for the infant to deal with its extreme helplessness and the anxiety of persecution which is experienced at this point in development. Therefore, the infant must split in order to survive. It is also important to note here that the good breast, for Klein, is seen as the locus of creativity. She sees "...the breast in its good aspect (as) the prototype of maternal goodness, inexhaustible patience and generosity, as well as of creativeness" (Klein, 1975 B, p. 180). If these good experiences begin to outweigh the bad, the ego or self can begin to be constructed out of an essentially alive and creative element in the breast. Klein calls this phase of development the "paranoid-schizoid position" and locates it in the first three months of life.

As development proceeds after the first three months, a dramatic shift seems to take place; the infant is able to experience more than the circumscribed world of the breast in its various aspects or parts. The infant then begins to emerge into a relationship with the whole of the mother's body and into the beginnings of a relationship with the larger world. The leading anxiety in the shift from part to whole object also shifts from persecutory anxiety to fear of the loss of the loved object, now experienced as a whole and all-encompassing world for the infant. The essence of this fear of loss is that the child's own destructive and sadistic impulses will drive the loved object away. Working through this "depressive position," as Klein calls it, is a process of keeping the destructive, sadistic impulses under control by diminishing the intensity of the conflict between love and aggression. The task for the infant is to build up the good objects within himself.

While splitting was the defensive manoeuvre employed in the earlier "paranoid-schizoid position," the infant now uses reparation as a major defense against the anxiety of loss in the "depressive position." Reparation is the process by which the ego tries to make restitution for all the sadistic attacks it has launched on the object (Klein, 1975 A, p. 265). Real experiences of the absence of mother and particularly of weaning stimulate dread of the loss of the internal object. Dread of the loss of the object, then, is directly linked to anxiety which comes from having split the object into parts. In the depressive position, the task is to bring all of these parts together into the experience of a whole which encompasses and can hold both good and bad.

The occurrence of the depressive position is central in terms of understanding the role of symbol-formation and creativity in connection with development. In the working through of the depressive position, reparation as the healing of the split object becomes the impulse to create. Sparing the object means integrating it by redirecting one's energies on to other substitute (symbolic) objects.

The concept of phantasy performs a unifying function for Klein. Because she postulates the existence of an ego from birth, Klein also maintains that the infant phantasizes its world from the very beginning, since the ego is the source of phantasy. Driven by the instincts and anxiety over its helplessness, the infant will alternate between phantasies about the good breast (good, satisfying, milk-giving) and the bad breast (dry, empty, withholding). These repeated experiences with the breast will give rise to further phantasies: either the infant will enjoy the breast and experience pleasure and gratitude or its frustration will lead to persecutory feelings and will cause it to want to destroy the breast, to scoop it out and devour it.

Phantasy can then be seen as a mediation between the infant's experience of the demands of its own body and its experience of how those demands are responded to in the external world. The infant's phantasies as instinctual representatives are ways of bringing outside to inside and inside to outside. The splitting of good and bad breast in phantasy is a defensive manoeuvre designed to protect the infant from being overwhelmed by the initial experience of chaos and anxiety both inside and outside itself. Phantasy, in Klein's view, is not a retreat from reality but is, rather, the bridge to reality for the infant. The content of phantasy shifts as the infant's ego develops. In the depressive position, when the ego is capable of perceiving a whole object (parent) and not merely a part object (breast), the phantasies are concerned with ambivalence about separation from the whole loved object. Omnipotent phantasies and phantasies of destruction lead to guilt and the desire to make up for destructive wishes. In sparing the loved objects, the infant has to control and diminish its impulses. It is in this space of the depressive position that symbolic formations can arise.

My point here is to show that the capacity to phantasize paves the way for further developments such as creative expression and artistic activity by serving as a bridge between internal demands and experiences and the demands and experiences of the outside world. Phantasy pushes the infant toward the object world. In the first six months of life, according to Klein, a whole series of internal and external experiences are processed by the infant in phantasy. These clusters of phantasies then pave the way for more highly developed capacities: curiosity about the world and its contents, the ability to learn, to create and to re-create.

Lighting the Fire: Illusion, Transitional Space and Primary Creativity

D.W. Winnicott's work builds upon this notion of the creation of illusion as a precondition of imaginative activity.
Winnicott was concerned with understanding the development
of the infant in terms of the link between creativity and the building up of self and world. His work dovetails with Klein's and
reflects her influence upon him. Between 1935 and 1940, she
was his supervisor. Winnicott's interest in psychoanalysis grew
out of his work as a paediatrician; and as he moved away from
the practice of paediatrics, he retained a focus on therapeutic
consultations with children while seeing adult patients as well.

What led Winnicott to use Klein's theoretical framework as
a touchstone was her emphasis upon the mother/infant matrix
in the constitution of the self and the world. In addition to
this focus upon the mother/infant relationship, Winnicott was
especially impressed with Klein's discussion of the depressive
position in terms of its place in normal, healthy development
as well as its role in the integration of the self. It is in the
depressive position that the infant experiences him or herself
as whole and the mother as whole and sustaining. This provides the ground for a number of enriching developmental
moves: the ability to tolerate aggressive feelings toward the
mother, the ability to experience guilt and the desire to make
up to the mother (reparation).

Weaning is generally associated with the flowering of the
depressive position. The mother's stance shifts from the actual
holding of the infant to what Winnicott calls the mother holding "...a situation in time" (Winnicott, 1975, p. 267). Here the
mother stands quietly by while the baby excitedly experiments
and takes risks meeting the consequences. What Winnicott calls
good enough mothering and *a good enough or facilitating environment* provide the assurance that whatever happens, the
mother and the world will survive. Good enough mothering
and good enough environment are repeatedly responsive to the

needs of the infant, fostering in the infant a sense of being real and responded to on all levels.

The good-enough mother is relatively successful at adapting to the infant's gestures and needs. This comes about long before the baby is born, when in pregnancy the mother is primarily preoccupied and capable of a strong identification with her unborn child:

> This essential maternal function enables the mother to know about her infant's earliest expectations and needs, and makes her personally satisfied in so far as the infant is at ease. It is because of this identification with her infant that she knows how to hold her infant, so that the infant starts by existing and not by reacting (Winnicott, 1965, p. 148).

The good enough mother provides the infant with the experience of the feeling of omnipotence. That is, she allows the baby to feel held together so that he or she is able to find and come to terms with the object as presented by the mother. This gives the baby the feeling of having created these objects. At the very beginning, the mother fosters the illusion that her breast is part of the infant and under the infant's magical control, that the breast is created by the infant out of his or her capacity to love and to need. The mother's breast is, then, a subjective experience of the infant:

> The mother places the actual breast just where the infant is ready to create, and at the right moment (Winnicott, 1971, p. 13).

The infant then has the illusion that the external world or reality corresponds to his or her own *capacity to create.* Yet alongside the necessary fostering of illusion, the good enough mother also disillusions the infant. This process of disillusionment refers to inevitable periods of separation and moments of frustration which are sprinkled throughout the infant's experience. It may also refer to the times when mother and infant are out-of-tune such that the baby momentarily may feel let-down or dropped by the mother:

If things go well in this gradual disillusionment process, the stage is set for the frustrations that gather together under the word weaning; but it should be remembered that when we talk about the phenomena that cluster around weaning we are assuming the underlying process, the process by which opportunity for illusion and gradual disillusionment is provided (Winnicott, 1971, p. 15).

Out of this matrix of illusion and disillusion comes the notion of the *transitional object* and, more generally, of *transitional space*. This notion of a transitional area of experience which emerges from earliest times is a major contribution to our understanding of human development, especially in relation to the origins of creative, imaginal experience. It is important for our purposes now to explore this concept in more depth.

Winnicott derived the concept of the transitional object from his concrete observations of children and the patterns which he discerned around the use of what he called the first "not-me possession." The newborn infant's fist-in-mouth activities lead eventually to attachment to objects outside of the self. Yet these objects—teddy bear, blanket, doll—all carry a particular meaning for the child:

> The relationship which the child has with the transitional object occurs in an intermediate area where the child can exercise control. The child has rights over the object; it must never change or be changed; and it must survive loving and aggression directed toward it by the child (Winnicott, 1971, p. 6).

In this way, the child deals with the experience of loss and the disillusioning process by restoring the relation to the mother in the form of the transitional object. The transitional object provides an "intermediate area of experience" and restores the illusion of omnipotence, of oneness with the mother, by magical control.

In addition, the infant is beginning to recognize the distinction between internal and external worlds and create the transitional object as a container for the distinction, in-between the two worlds. It stands in-between infant and mother and stands for the interconnection between them at the same time:

> The object represents the infant's transition from a state of being merged with the mother to a state of being in relation to the mother as something outside and separate (Winnicott, 1971, p. 17).

Winnicott moves from the role played by the transitional object in building the relation between self and world in infancy to a broader examination of the transitional object as providing the first opportunity for the experience of symbolic activity. The transitional object and transitional phenomena, according to Winnicott, create a space which is the potential locus of play, creativity, and cultural experience in general:

> This intermediate area of experience, unchallenged in respect of its belonging to inner or external (shared) reality, constitutes the greater part of the infant's experience, and throughout life is retained in the intense experiencing that belongs to the arts and to religion and to imaginative living and to creative scientific work (Winnicott, 1971, p. 16).

The transitional object retains its aliveness and symbolic character because it participates in a continuous flow between the absence and the renewed presence of the object. The transitional object temporarily fills up the absences. It is an absent-presence and as such can be a field or container for all kinds of imaginative activity. In fact, in order to be of value it must be used imaginatively. Failure to use or take up this transitional space disrupts self-formation and can have serious consequences. One such consequence would be the proclivity to develop what Winnicott calls the "false self." In this type of self-organization, a person would be over-compliant, feel unreal or empty and be filled with a sense of futility. In extreme cases, there is such a split between true self (real, creative, authentic) and false self that:

> Instead of cultural pursuits one observes in such persons extreme restlessness, an inability to concentrate, and a need to collect impingements fom external reality so that the living-time of the individual can be filled by

reactions to these impingements (Winnicott, 1965. p. 150).

The sense of aliveness and its relation to creativity and transitional space is crucial here. Winnicott is speaking about *primary creativity* which emerges from the mother/infant dyad but which also is a creativity born from bodily experience. In his discussion of the first appearance of play as it is fundamentally connected to creativity, we get a sense of the connection of creativity, play and the body. Winnicott speaks of a sequence of relationships related to the developmental unfolding of the capacity to play. He divides this sequence into four stages or moments. First, baby and mother are merged, and mother creates the illusion that needs are met at the moment when the baby is ready to have them met (direct bodily satisfaction, immediate gratification). Then there emerges what Winnicott calls a "play-ground" between mother and baby. In the play-ground, there is a rudimentary sense of mutuality or back and forth, a sharing of images. The baby experiences both magical omnipotence in the potential space of relationship and the experience of actually being able to control or manipulate objects in the outer world—a sense of having an impact on the mother. Playing is now occurring and is exciting. It has a real charge because of "...the precariousness of the interplay of personal psychic reality and the experiences of control of actual objects" (Winnicott, 1974, p. 55).

This second stage gives over to a third which involves the capacity to be alone in the presence of the mother. Here what is required is some ability on the infant's part to hold the mother in mind as attending and interested when she is present but not directly paying attention to the child. The image of a good object (good enough mother) is inside of the baby in this stage. Reliable and trusted, it becomes available when needed. The final stage involves the ability of baby and mother to truly play together—in the overlap of two play areas. Here at first mother tries to fit in with the baby's play and follow it. Later, she introduces play of her own. A relationship is now formed in which both baby and mother share, bringing their own particular play with them into the "play-ground."

Thus, Winnicott shows that play emerges initially from the sense of illusion based upon bodily need and need satisfaction within the context of relationship. Because play and creativity are interconnected, he locates the origins of creativity in physical experience that is played out initially in the earliest relationship of life. The child comes into the world with a sense of aliveness, an assertive/aggressive "primary creativity" which is an expression of its very existence. If the environment can "hold" this primary creativity, then the child's capacity for creative expression in the world will have been established.

This concept of primary creativity distinguishes Winnicott's view from Klein's. Because of her adherence to Freud's concept of the death instinct, Klein sees aggression as a destructive attack upon the mother's body. Creativity, for her, is then understood as a defense against the persecutory anxiety which this aggression calls forth. Therefore, although Klein does lay the groundwork for understanding the role of phantasy in the development of the self, she nevertheless views creativity as a defensive manoeuvre. For Winnicott, on the other hand, the child enters the world with a fundamental assertion of its right to be alive, to be itself. This assertion of its own existence has an aggressive component, but this very aggressiveness is part of its creative being. Thus, for Winnicott, creativity is not a defense against anxiety but the very expression of existence itself. To be alive is to be creative.

The formation of a transitional realm of experience is only possible on the ground of this primary creativity with which the infant enters the world. If the mother can provide a good-enough environment to hold the child's expression of its existence, then the child will be capable of moving into transitional space. Winnicott's notion of transitional space provides a key to understanding the necessity of an experience of the blurring of the edges between the inner and outer worlds. Thus, he helps us comprehend the importance of transitional experience in the life of the developing infant as a basis for creative expression. In showing how this experience forms the foundation of a creative relationship between self and world, he has provided us with a rich source of inspiration for our work in the expressive arts therapies.

Tending the Fire:
Psychotherapy and the Arts

We have explored thus far the way in which phantasy is dynamically interconnected with the building up of a primary sense of creativity, emerging out of the earliest bodily experiences of the mother/breast/infant. We have also seen how in the early experiences of the infant a transitional space is built up which depends upon an illusion of absence-presence. The establishment of this transitional space makes the capacity for play and, subsequently, art-making possible.

Once creativity has been built up and kindled in the psyche, it must also be tended or attended to. This attending is essential for creativity to continue to be a force in development. Tending the fire means a kind of caretaking of this sense of art/play/creativity within transitional space, helping the child to retain a sense of aliveness. Unfortunately, as a culture, we have not been successful in tending to the creativity of children, particularly as they enter the educational process. Many children begin to lose a connection to their creativity early on. Certainly our current school structure with its emphasis upon instrumental learning and achievement mitigates against the fostering of creativity. Allowing children to play lasts only until the beginning of primary school; even in kindergarten there is a growing emphasis upon acquiring skills such as reading and mathematics. Not too many teachers are interested in letting children "fool around" or explore widely, collapsing the boundaries between subject areas—i.e., using drama to explore relationships, using art to learn mathematical concepts, teaching reading by allowing first graders to write and tell stories in their own way. This type of teaching requires time and skills not often taught in teacher training. Often teachers are under pressure to teach the curriculum and get through certain material. Parents also have expectations of their children in terms of future careers and competition. As a result, play is shaped to fit into this general mentality. Play gets relegated to the school yard at recesstime; even there children may play games which are goal-directed and literal rather than circular or phantasy-based.

Later on, if we develop performing arts schools or curricula, they seem to emphasize the performance aspects of the arts. These kind of schools encourage emerging adolescent artists to compete against each other for "star" status rather than to revel in and to enjoy both their own creative process and the process of co-creating with others who have creative fire. If we manage to remain connected to the arts as adults, we are often preoccupied with "making it" as artists and sometimes, of necessity, with selling our creative skills in the marketplace where the product is tailored for consumption.

Most adults who are not artists seem to have lost the spark entirely. I have worked with many people over time who say that they cannot do art, that they are not "good" at it. They are terrified to try anything for fear of failure. This sense of being judged seems to come in large part from bad experiences in art classes in school where the teacher was constantly critical of their products: "This doesn't look like a house. Do it over the *right* way." Messages like this ultimately lead to the abandonment of art or to viewing it as something special reserved for a select few. This attitude also leads to the sense that art is something set apart, only to be experienced in the context of museums, galleries, and performances in which people are spectators at a distance. Certainly they are not participants.

Placed in a broader cultural context, the emergence of the expressive arts therapies can be seen as an attempt to re-energize the whole area of creativity in our experience. This development stands as an antidote to the forces of culture which have damped down creative energy and made ordinary individuals feel uncomfortable with this aspect of themselves. A major premise of the use of the arts in therapy is that all of us can connect with the creative fire. What I have been trying to show thus far is that we can all connect at this level precisely because, in terms of development, creativity was an essential source of our earliest experiences and helped to build a sense of relatedness to self and world, Thus, a theory of expressive arts therapy can acquire depth by drawing upon the way in which psychoanalysis roots development in a basic connection to creativity as emerging from the earliest bodily relationships of self and other. This connection is both fundamental and universal.

Therapy can be seen as one way in which the fire of creativity is tended, particularly a therapy which has the arts as its focus and uses the arts as a mediating force for the therapeutic project. In my view, expressive arts therapy rests upon a double foundation. On the one hand, it derives much of its impetus from the discipline of the arts. The idea of a theory of expressive arts therapy which has its roots in artistic practice needs to be developed. We will make an effort in this direction in the latter part of this section. The other foundational aspect of my work lies in the psychoanalytic tradition. I have been developing these concepts in order to show the way in which creativity, the focus of expressive arts therapy, can be understood to be a critical building block of the self. As we have seen, creative energy is fundamental to relationship and has its origins in our earliest bodily experiences. The fire of creativity is built right away, as soon as we enter the world; and it is lit as soon as we begin to relate to others. It is fed by early experiences in which others respond to our aliveness. The act of tending the fire is crucial to keeping the creative force alive in the self.

The transitional space is an area of vitality where creativity finds its home. To the extent that they promote creativity and vitality, the task of the arts therapies is to encourage the flowering of a transitional area of experience. Perhaps we could call this area the "fire-place." A theory of expressive arts therapy needs to account for the ways in which this fire-place is formed.

Shaping, Giving Form and the Holding Environment

Expressive arts therapy uses the disciplines of the arts to give particular shape and form to experience. This shaping of experience into an artistic form provides the container, holding environment or transitional space of the therapeutic relationship.

Thus, the visual images in painting hold the internal world of the artist but in an external form. The choreography of the dance shapes space and holds in concrete form the inner experience of the dancer. The tone of the music gives form to the experience of the musician. Poetic speech gives shape to that which cannot be expressed through a linear discourse. The creation of the stage as a frame around inner experience perpetuates the outer drama.

In order for shape and form to gather together into a particular artistic container, experience must begin in formlessness. Before the dance can emerge, there is play and experimentation with many different possibilities. Likewise, before the poem takes its shape on the page, many images need to be tried and discarded along the way. Improvisations in creating the drama help to free up the process and allow the final form to emerge. To really play at this stage means to give up any sense of a fixed idea of what will happen or of knowing anything beforehand. This attitude of letting go must be practiced and cultivated. It comes more easily to some than to others. Entering the chaos of formlessness and letting go can be frightening. Order, structure or form for experience thus needs to emerge organically out of playful experimentation. Beginning to shape the work of art with a preconceived notion of its outcome cuts off creativity and is another way to flatten the images.

The expressive arts therapist thus helps to create a space in which images are invited and in which they are served. This requires an understanding on many levels: an understanding of the artistic process and artistic techniques as well as of psychotherapeutic practice and its application to individuals, groups, and communities. The particular way in which this complex of understanding is translated into the practice of expressive arts therapy must be sure to keep images at the focus of attention. Images, whether from visual art, dance, music, drama or poetry, are the containers which also carry the work forward. By engaging in the discipline of the arts, keeping creation of the image, its refinement and elaboration at the focus of the therapeutic frame, a therapeutic effect can be provided.

The process of engaging with images and entering the imaginal frame by means of the discipline of the arts is essential to understanding the therapeutic action of expressive arts therapy. If we combine this perspective with the notion of transitional space and the holding environment coming from Winnicott, we add an important dimension to our work. Essential to Winnicott's concept is the creative process as it is rooted in bodily experience—the earliest relationship of the infant to the mother's body. In order for it to have an effect, the therapeutic relationship must maintain a sense of vitality and encourage the emergence of vitality in the patient. This is precisely the process of tending the fire. It is done by nurturing the artistic process and inviting it to come into the therapeutic space— we do this by recognizing the role of the arts in creating a transitional area of experience.

Being Moved

Play and the use of the body are essential to expressive arts therapy. These are elements, as well, in the early building blocks of creativity embedded in the mother/infant interaction. Mother and infant move in response to each other. In this inter-action, each one moves and is moved. The sense of being moved is thus essential for expressive arts therapy. Creating something aesthetically moving comes out of play and the body. Knill, Barba, and Fuchs, in their book, *Minstrels of Soul* (1995), speak about the aesthetic response and aesthetic response-ability as key to the understanding of the action of expressive therapy. We have to have a sense of awe that takes our breath away as we witness artistic work that comes from the deepest aspects of the self. This could be likened to the mirroring function in the mother/infant dyad where vitality is flowing back and forth. But it is also bound up with an aesthetics that enters therapeutic work with the arts: we want to make things that are beautiful and that move us to a new emotional place.

An *aesthetic response*...refers to a distinct response, with a bodily origin, to an occurrence in the imagination, to an artistic act, or to the perception of an art work. When the response is profound and soul-stirring, we describe it as "moving" or "breath-taking" *(Atem-beraubend)*. Our language suggests a sensory effect associated with the image, what Hillman describes as revealing itself in the quick in-breath (or *inspiration*) we might experience when in the presence of beauty... (Knill, et al. 1995, p. 71).

Action and Expression

Although we have worked through psychoanalytic theory to find the roots of creative action in the world, we cannot rely on psychoanalytic practice as an adequate foundation for expressive arts therapy. This practice uses metaphorical speech and the shaping of the relationship between patient and analyst by means of *the word*, while expressive arts therapy practice is based upon *action*, a doing rather than a speaking-about. The word and language are essential expressive tools; but they are seen from this perspective as one among other expressive forms and not necessarily the dominant ones. Art-making in the context of expressive arts therapy may or may not take place through speech unless the purpose of the speech or text is to enhance the imaginal aspects of the work. Poetic speech and storytelling are the preferred forms of the word. As much as possible, any *talking about* which might tend to deaden the process is discouraged. What we encourage is activity which expands and elaborates through image-making. In this way, the work becomes more authentic and has a deeper quality.

Playing with Images

Thus expressive arts therapy rests on the notion that we need to get out of the way and allow the images to come through. The artistic disciplines provide us with methods, techniques and a way of seeing which, in turn, are the pathways for the images to follow. In free painting sessions, for example, where the emphasis is upon relaxation and spontaneity, often startling and vivid images come forward. There is a sense of surprise and wonder: How did I do that? Where did that come from? To work with or, rather, play with the images in order to bring them forward and to understand the messages/gifts that they are carrying is central to our work. Talking about images can tend to flatten them or make them less available aesthetically. Perhaps it is because we move from the imaginal rooted in the body up into the conceptual which can become detached from the body. We need to play with the images so that they remain fresh and alive, coming from the sources of primary creativity rooted in the body.

One technique designed to work with images to retain their aliveness is that of dialoguing with the images, playing with them in an imaginative way.   Here the image is personified—it is not a thing out-there but taken to be a living being which has an independent existence. In a sense, images are thus conceived of as children: we give birth to them but we do not own them. They live outside of us and are not reflections of ourselves. Playing with the images here means speaking directly to it as "you."   We then shift perspective and speak as the image, addressing the one who was the creator. This shift of focus can often be an important factor in creating a new understanding emerging from the perspective of the image. In and of itself, the technique is imaginal and therefore inviting and playful—it is experimental and explorative.

Shaun McNiff has led the way for us in the development of this approach. In his book, *Art As Medicine (1992),* he talks about becoming a listener to what the painting has to say:

> When I perceive the painting that I make, or the dream that I have as other than myself, I set the stage for dialogue. The painting might have something to say to me, and so I take on the role of listener rather than explainer. A shift takes place in art therapy when people leave the ego postion and let the figures in paintings speak through them....Fresh and intriguing statements

are made. The person speaking is taken by surprise. A sense of vitality emerges from these spontaneous expressions, unrestrained by habitual explanations. Getting out of the ego voice and experiencing other perspectives are fundamental to conflict resolution, innovation, and productivity (McNiff, 1992, p. 106).

Images emerge from the transitional space of play rooted in bodily interaction; to play with these images brings out their vital source.

Distancing

Dialoguing with the image points to another essential feature in work with the arts in therapy—distancing. What can make work with the arts more interesting and inviting is the fact that the artist/patient is not talking directly about the self but, rather, encountering aspects of the self through a mediating process which allows for a space containing both self and not-self. Distancing allows for the capacity to separate and externalize, not to detach but to maintain a connection without fusion. The visual image, for example, can be seen as a crystallization of feelings in the form of the art work, not the actual feelings themselves. In this way, the image can be encountered as a semi-independent reality. There is often a comfort in this kind of distancing; it can be much less overwhelming. Thus it creates a space within the psyche for understanding and re-incorporation (taking it back into the body).

One might think that distancing mitigates against the tending of the fire, that in the process of mediating feelings by means of the art work, intensity is lost. In fact, the distancing function of the work of art serves the image by allowing for more room to explore. By playing with the art work, one can create a more intense relationship to it. There is a sense of freedom in making art that one does not necessarily feel when simply expressing feelings directly. The form that begins to take shape out-there is no longer just an extension of the self, a mirror. One has the opportunity to refine the image over and over until it is a crystallization of the essence of the feeling. Because it is out-there at a distance from the self, it can also speak to others. In order for the image to have value, it must provoke a response in an other.

Any use of the arts in therapy provides a distancing function due to the creation of transitional space in art-making. However, there are certain techniques which explicitly make use of the distancing function. Role play, in addition to dialoguing with images, is a good example of such a technique. Here, through words, actions, or movements, a radical shift in perspective takes place in which roles are reversed and reversed again. Enacting the point of view of the other and feeling what this is like involves new information and, on a deeper level, a new bodily experience. Role play also brings the relationship alive to otherness, providing an opportunity for playful pretending and imaginative elaboration. By creating an as-if situation in play, there is the possiblity for exploration and, as always, surprise. There is a significant felt difference between talking about a difficult or conflictual relationship with an other person or part of the self and *being* the other for a discrete period of time—talking, walking, and feeling the experience of otherness.

Intermodality as the Creation of Pathways

Expressive arts therapy technique has at its foundation the notion of the *intermodal* nature of artistic activity—literally inter or between modalities. This notion is essential to understanding the whole project of expressive arts therapy. No one single artistic form can crystallize every feeling; moreover, each individual has a different style of expression. It is through the interpenetration of the arts that expression can go deeper, becoming a more authentic presentation of the self. In terms of dialoguing with images, for example, often there is interpenetration of the arts involved—using poetic speech, visual art, movement and dramatic enactment.

Role-play might thus emerge from the crystallization of feeling in a painting. Two forces are in conflict in the imagery. They are then brought forward and enacted. Or it might be an extension of work being done in dance where two energies need to change places and experience how that feels. This is an example of the concept of the *intermodal transfer*, described by Knill (1995). Here the image is brought forward by means of movement from one artistic form into another. Not only is the image coming forward but the entire process is deepening.

In this emphasis upon extending and deepening images, a major underlying rationale for the use of intermodal transfer becomes clear. Images are the tools that we work with in expressive arts therapy; it is important to receive them in the proper way. In her essay, "Six Approaches to the Image in Art Therapy" (1981), Mary Watkins discusses various stances toward images in our culture, particularly therapeutic stances toward images. In general, she finds that we tend to want to manipulate images in some way: either we use them for diagnostic purposes (goal-directed use of images), or we regard them as dangerous and promoting disintegration in the patient, or we see them as instruments of treatment which themselves need to be healed (transformed from destructive to ego-enhancing); or we interpret them and get rid of them; or we make no attempt to understand them at all. The sixth stance which Watkins suggests is that of trusting in the images and allowing them to reveal themselves in whatever way they need to. As therapists we can inquire into the meaning of the images but only through the form of other images. In this way, we keep the images flowing at the same time as we are seeking to understand them.

This process necessarily leads us to provide as many avenues for the images as possible. There cannot be only one way in which an image manifests itself. Different pathways are also important for the process of reflection upon the image.

An image has a totality to it, such that one part calls out to another. A certain character could only have one kind of room to live in, or tone of voice with which he speaks. In a drawing when one part of an image emerges, often a question allows the rest to unfold:

Where does this take place? What time of day is it? What does the air feel like? What is the atmosphere of this place? Who is present? What happens here? What just happened? Where are you in relation to this scene? If the picture is of a person, one might ask what he/ she is thinking about, where he/she is, where one is in relation to the figure. One might ask what seems familiar about the person or the mood around the person. One can suggest that the painter step inside the picture, into the place or into a relation with the figure depicted. But always the focus is on the image (Watkins, 1981, p. 124).

In one group where the theme was the shaping of each person's space in both movement and visual art, members of the group began with a long movement exploration which resulted in the creation of a movement phrase. Then the group moved over (transferred) to painting with big brushes in one color on large pieces of paper. An attempt was made to retain the felt-sense of the movement phrase and translate this into paint. Then, after a time of free painting using many colors, the new images which resulted were reincorporated by transferring them back to a new movement phrase or set of phrases. In the end, group members explored in pairs what happens when two movement phrases encounter each other. The movement interaction produced yet another image which was the synthesis of various elements of the separate phrases. In performances at the end, one was able to observe this process and to see it crystallized in an artistic form—the dance. The intermodal transfer thus enhanced the images which themselves became pieces of the dance construction. This construction emerged out of personal expression coming together to create a whole dance structure with the effect of moving and touching others, creating an aesthetic response.

Transferring from one art modality to another or between modalities keeps the image from flattening and reveals more meanings as the transfers proceed. Transfer perpetuates transformation: the image is constructed and then deconstructed over and over in a cyclical fashion. Playing with the images by continuing to transform them artistically recapitulates the circular quality of playing itself. Expressive arts therapy, then, takes place on the play-ground where all creative work occurs.

The transfer is also a form of inquiry, an uncovering of meanings which takes place as we go around and around from one art form to another. The image comes forward and is deepened. As it does so, we begin to understand more about the image. As it goes around, it is changed. When a movement phrase is translated into painting, something new emerges which, when taken back into movement, changes yet again. There is a kind of clarification that occurs, and, at times, one can get to the *essence* of a theme or a feeling in this way.

In a group comprised of adolescents, for example, we made clay fantasy creatures. After constructing these imaginary beasts, we told stories about them which were then enacted by members of the group. The story came alive and was transformed by the activity of the participants; it was not simply a literal acting-out of the text. Each participant put his or her interpretation on the role they were playing and therefore enhanced the image of the whole. The storywriters were amazed at the directions that were suggested by the imaginations of the participants and at the meanings which emerged ultimately when the whole was constructed. The story thus left the domain of the purely personal and became, in a sense, everyone's story, a collective imaginal creation. This process could happen because we began with the individual creation and then moved out to a group form and because we took the image further by means of different art modalities—from visual art to expressive language to drama.

Art-in-Relationship

Another crucial aspect of the work of expressive arts therapy is the role of *relationship* in the process. Expressive arts therapy is essentially relational in its approach. This brings us back again to the notions of transitional phenomena and the transitional area of experience with which we began. On almost every level, there is a relational aspect to this work. First, in terms of making art at all, one has a relationship to the materials which are in space out-there. One encounters the materials and interacts with them to produce the art work. Making art in the context of a relationship of patient to therapist adds yet another relational aspect. Now relation to the materials takes place within the context of the relationship between the therapist and patient, a relationship which is also in the mediated area or transitional space—both me and not-me. Patient and therapist are working together in the third area, that of the in-between space. They are creating it together both in terms of their relationship itself as an art work and in terms of the actual works of art that find their place there.

Response is crucial. Not only does the therapist receive the images and invite them to come forward by means of a nonjudgmental attitude, she also gives feedback—a response which itself takes the inquiry with the image to a new place. The therapist serves the image by interacting with the patient through the imaginal or transitional realm. At times the therapist might take the lead with her own images, at other times it is the patient who is leading. Both are doing so within the frame of the therapy relationship. In this relationship, as in any therapeutic relationship, the parameters still exist: we still pay attention to issues in transference and countertransference, to boundaries.   But we do so with an awareness that boundaries are not fixed, that the therapeutic work takes place in the area where our boundaries meet and overlap.

In work with groups, interaction is paramount, and the notion of response/feedback is central. In expressive art therapy groups, when conflict emerges, for example, one way in which the therapist might work with it would be to call for an expressive inventory: each member names what they are feeling in an artistic way. Then the group creates a response to these namings, either as a whole or in pairs. This response acknowledges what members are feeling and allows them to be seen and heard. Yet putting the responses into an artistic form transforms them at the same time. The artistic shaping of conflictual feeling might provide an opportunity to dis-engage from the feeling and look at it with more distance as more out-there than in-here. There is a process of dis-identification which takes place when the images are externalized in artistic forms. This dis-identification promotes a clearer response.

In groups, responses are happening all the time, even if they are not explicitly named. In her book, *Group Interactive Art Therapy (1993)*, Diane Waller discusses the concept of "resonance" which, borrowed from the science of acoustics, aptly describes what happens in a group when each member begins to reverberate with events or with what is happening to someone else. In a group where art-making occurs, images as well as people can resonate with each other:

> Resonance occurs when each member of a group responds to a stimulating input (such as the impending group break) so that the group as a whole becomes highly charged with energy. Very powerful emotions may be evoked—for example, a theme of separation may emerge in a group, evoking powerful responses in each member who produces his or her own material relevant to separation or avoidance of it. Thus the member 'resonates' to the group theme at his or her natural frequency (Waller, 1993, p. 15).

Images certainly can resonate with each other both positively and negatively. In one training group, there had been a great deal of conflict for some time. Finally, in one session, the group was able to create a painting together which seemed to provide them with a sense of harmony and cohesiveness. They spoke to the painting, in dialogue fashion, expressing deep feelings of love and appreciation to the image. As they were experiencing a period of respite from the storming of the past, one member approached the image and tore a long strip of it down the middle, saying that she needed to create a space in the image/group for herself, that she was not experiencing the group as a loving or harmonious place. Some members of the group were extremely upset and felt violated by this action. Others could allow for this expression. There was much discussion about the ethics of the situation—did she have a right to encroach on the image in this way without asking permission? After this, some group members ripped the image further and took bits and pieces of it for their own journals, perhaps wanting to preserve the good feeling from the image as a whole. These bits, as deconstructions, were then synthesized into new images and given new meanings. This experience of resonance left traces in the group for some time afterwards and gave rise to many new and interesting although painful images.

The relationship which develops in therapeutic work with the discipline of the arts is more of a circular than a linear one. Resonance implies a back and forth movement. Introducing play into the relationship necessitates circularity: play is not goal-directed behaviour.   Patient and therapist are looking together, searching together for forms which emerge out of an experience of playing-around. They are actually playing-around together as a mutual inquiry: What can happen here? What form will it take? Margot Fuchs (unpublished material) refers to the therapeutic relationship as artistic re-searching:

> allow
> the forming
> to be
> with the not yet formed
> allow
> the forming
> to be
> with the formed
> and
> the de-formed
>
> the formed
> the de-formed
> the forming
> the to be formed
> the not yet formed
> trans-
> FORM-
> ation

creating
by going
through
and
with

In this section, I have attempted to show the ways in which the practice of expressive arts therapy can be rooted in psychoanalytic theory. I have focused here on understanding the role of creativity in the development of the self and how creative inspiration needs to be tended in order for living to maintain vitality. The focal concept which has come from the psychoanalytic perspective is that of transitional space. It is in this space that creativity resides and creative activities find their home. It is the experience of transitional space that is fostered by expressive arts therapy.

At the same time that expressive arts therapy connects in significant ways to the psychoanalytic project, we can see ways in which it departs and diverges as well. When we add art-making to the therapeutic process, we add a whole new set of concepts to the mix. What we add are more ways to tend the fire, more ways to extend and deepen the experience of transitional space. As expressive arts therapists, we need to practice our work with the idea that we are fire-tenders—helping people to connect and reconnect with the creativity that is a basic element of existence in the world. As we have seen, creativity emerges in the earliest experience of self-body-other relationship. For this reason, we need to pay attention to the therapeutic relationship as a transitional area which allows for creativity to flower.

Our job is to re-ignite and feed the fire, making sure that it does not go out. We do this by means of the arts: beginning in formlessness and play, finding shape and form through the holding container of an artistic process. The art-work finds its home in the transitional area of experience—that which is both me and not-me. The art-work, as distanced from the self, creates both a response in the self and in others who are witness to it. Because of its intermodal nature, expressive arts therapy makes use of all the arts in order to maintain the aliveness of the image. Intermodal technique serves the image, helping to crystallize feeling into form. This form can be manifold: a dance, a sculpture, a painting, a piece of music, a story, a poem, a dramatic enactment or combinations of all of these modes. It is by transferring the image from one modality into the other that the imaginal is enriched and enhanced. Perhaps our job as therapists is done when those with whom we work are able to tend their own fires, recognizing the importance of creativity and practicing it in their everyday lives.

This is the very problem of creative life: how to
have a future while not forgetting the past? how to
ensure that passion be made luminous without
being cooled?.....What I recognize to be living—
living in the immediate sense—is what I recognize
as being hot. Heat is the proof par excellence of
substantial richness and permanence: it alone gives
an immediate meaning to vital intensity, to intensity
of being.

Gaston Bachelard, *The Psychoanalysis of Fire*

PART THREE

Working with Fire: The Practice of Expressive Arts Therapy

Introduction

In this part of the book, I write about the practice of expressive arts therapy. For the reader to understand my practical work better, it might be helpful to begin with an account of my own training and education. I began with a five year training at the Toronto Art Therapy Institute in the early 1970's. The theoretical framework used at the Institute was classically psychoanalytic: understanding art images as symbolic of unconscious, primary processes. The task of the art therapist was conceived of as eliciting the patient's associations to art work and attempting to construct meanings from them in the form of insights. The work was created in an atmosphere of openness and in a non-judgmental frame, with the patient being encouraged to relax and to be as spontaneous as possible with the materials. While I felt that this training was a good introduction to the field of art therapy, I became particularly fascinated with the world of childhood through my practica and wanted to focus my work more in that direction.

I then entered another five year training in child analysis in the Toronto Child Psychotherapy Program. In this training, new directions in psychoanalytic theory, such as object-relations and self-psychology, were incorporated. I also began to work with expanding the transitional frame to include not only the arts but also play and phantasy. I experienced the richness of working in this space and the excitement of encouraging images to come forward in whatever form they needed to take. Following the child's lead and providing possibilities was, in itself, a kind of intermodal practice; although at this point in my training, I had not yet conceptualized this connection.

In order to connect the two trainings, art therapy and child psychotherapy, I used the opportunity of my doctoral thesis at York University to explore the theoretical implications of using the arts in therapy and how the symbolic dimension of our experience can have a therapeutic function. I found Winnicott's notion of transitional space to be crucial in understanding the imaginal world of the arts and in the kind of exploration and experimentation necessary for undertaking therapeutic work.

In 1984 and 1985, I spent my time practicing a mixture of art and child psychotherapy on Martha's Vineyard and in Cambridge, MA. It was during this period that I met the faculty in the Institute for the Arts and Human Development at Lesley College Graduate School: particularly, Paolo Knill, Shaun McNiff, Elizabeth McKim, and Stan Strickland. These highly creative and original people impressed me with their sense of aliveness and the connections that they were making between the arts and therapy. At this time, there was a sense of community that they had built around themselves. It was exciting just to be there and to get a taste of this feast.

Returning to Toronto in 1986, I faced an inner emptiness. I felt disconnected and isolated, having been away and out of things for two years. I was not terribly happy about returning. Depression had set in and, in desperation, I decided to take an intensive course in clowning. At most, I thought that it might make me laugh a bit. As I became immersed in this theatrical form and learned the discipline of clown, I began to move out of the depressive place and feel more alive. I began to experience the power of clown as an intermodal expressive arts therapy. The training involved dropping into the void, improvisation, and spontaneity, coupled with specific artistic disciplines such as movement, mask-making, painting, voice and text. Structures were suggested which encouraged the fostering of innocence and vulnerability—for example, making a home/a safe place, saying goodbye to a loved one, mask-making in clay with eyes closed.

I began making connections between the clown work and a therapy which begins in formlessness and follows images. Clown seemed like another art modality in which to explore and had potential to give experience yet another shape. After deepening my skills over time, I began to teach clowning with Steve Levine at the Easter Symposium, an annual gathering in Europe of expressive arts therapists from all over the world. The clown work provided a great deal of excitement. The experience of freedom that is possible in the clown form seemed to enliven people and to light their fires.

In the last four years, I have begun to train others in the theory and practice of expressive arts therapy as co-director of the ISIS-Canada training program. This experience has been a trial by fire and has further refined my skills. As a teacher and trainer, I have been challenged by the task of helping students learn to do expressive arts therapy not only in terms of acquiring basic skills but also in terms of developing a way of seeing themselves and others. I have tried to convey my excitement about this work to them and to excite them in turn. Accepting the inevitable doubt and despair, anger and pain as they manifest in the group process as well as in students' practicum experience has been essential and difficult for me. It has not only been a trial by fire but a refiner's fire as well on many levels. I feel stronger for it. The program continues to prod me to keep up my own creative work, to go regularly into the studio and to paint. Work needs to be kept from overwhelming all of my time. Playing at my work has been possible at ISIS as well. For this, I am grateful.

In this section of the book, I would like to explore some of the psychotherapeutic work that I have done over the past twenty years. This exploration will be done from the perspective that I have been developing in this book. I have brought expressive arts therapy into the agency where I have been working for the past eight years and incorporated the arts into my clinical work with individual children and with groups. Although there are restrictions in terms of space at the agency, there are no restrictions placed upon me regarding my practice of expressive arts therapy. I have found my colleagues to be receptive to this approach, even though none of them explicitly use the arts in their work.

There has always been a psychoanalytic stream at the agency, a number of staff whose work is guided and informed by a strong psychoanalytic framework. These colleagues are particularly supportive of the whole realm of play, art and fantasy, where much of their clinical interest lies as well. What has been most important for me is the sense that we connect theoretically and yet can accept our differences in terms of the way in which we carry out the theory in the practice of psychotherapy.

Over this period of working in the agency, from 1987 to the present, I have seen many children in individual therapy and have run several groups in addition to supervising trainees and participating in teaching seminars for the trainees. In this section, I will present and try to understand some of this clinical practice. What follows is practical work. I have chosen material that I think will be interesting to students and practitioners in the field of expressive arts therapy and to those who are intrigued by the way in which the arts open up new ways of seeing and keep the fire of creativity burning.

Creativity: Constriction and Containment

Farah began seeing me at the agency in September of 1988 when she was eleven years old. I have had contact with her, sometimes intensively and sometimes in a more attenuated way, until June, 1994. She is now seventeen years old.

In the initial assessment at the agency, Farah was seen as eager and able to engage. In the individual interview, which involved play interaction, she was a vivid storyteller with themes that had a common thread: people having animals in their care who died or were gotten rid of because they were too expensive to keep, too many of them, too much trouble or simply not fed. From this earliest play metaphor, many of Farah's issues emerged: separation, loss, lack of a sense of being cared for and lack of a sense of home.

In an interview, Mrs. B., her mother, was seen as preoccupied with her ex-husband and a failed marriage for which she felt personal responsibility and guilt. She felt that by divorcing, she had violated the strict religious beliefs of her Muslim culture. Mrs. B. felt angry and frustrated with Farah and also felt that she had not done her best for her. Mrs. B.'s need for attention and understanding for herself was quite apparent in the interview.

In the assessment formulation, the interviewers concluded that there were several important factors contributing to Farah's difficulties at the time: her birth into a tense marital situation, a needy and isolated mother who was self-preoccupied, and a disengaged father. In addition, many moves and separations had left Farah with little security in terms of a sense of belonging to one family or society and with a sense of anticipated displacement and rejection. Poor school performance was tending to heighten the sense of failure and of not belonging. Mrs. B.'s intense unresolved conflicts with her ex-husband were being acted out in the relationship with her daughter, who was identified in her mind with Mr. B.

Farah was seen as a young girl who, despite her difficulties, had some significant strengths. Connected to her vivid capacity for rich storytelling in play, Farah was also seen as likeable, creative, possessed of a lively imagination and highly expressive. However, after a course of family therapy in which Mrs. B. made the decision that, despite the fighting with Farah, she was committed to have her remain with her in Canada, the therapist began to feel that Farah's creativity was serving a more defensive function. Farah was isolated in her play; her drawing was more an attempt to ward off anxiety over abandonment and rejection than a free creative outlet. Farah's defiance toward her mother was also seen as a way of making contact with her mother, who was quite depressed most of the time. Fighting was negative, but at least they were engaging. For this reason, and because the family therapist was leaving the agency, she referred Farah to me for individual art therapy sessions in the hope that Farah would be able to free her creativity and use the art-making as a vehicle for her emerging self.

It was in this context that I began seeing Farah and her mother and sister to initially connect with the family. Mrs. B. was quite upset about the departure of the family therapist and had sent a dramatic letter of protest to the agency. This was my impression of Mrs. B.—outspoken, dramatic, and in turmoil emotionally. My first impression of Farah was how soft and delicate she seemed over and against her mother who was verbally so harsh with her. Farah reminded me of a fragile flower trying to establish itself in a hard and hostile soil. It was striking how much Mrs. B. favored Hala, Farah's sister, over Farah and said so quite openly and directly. Comparisons between Farah and Hala were made often, with Farah always coming out poorly. Mrs. B. had some notion that the separation from Farah for four years had contributed to her lack of connection with her daughter, but her insight about this fact did not seem to help her overcome her negative and hostile projections onto her eldest daughter.

I immediately felt empathy and compassion for Farah; my metaphor of the fragile flower was a powerful determinant in my connection to her. This metaphor often led me to want to protect her and to provide a nourishing emotional atmosphere for Farah which would be a counter-experience or corrective experience for her. I also felt quite challenged by Mrs. B. I was fascinated by her. She obviously had struggled through a great deal of pain in her life. She did want the best for her daughters, and she tried to form a connection to me in which she used me often as a co-parent. I tried to guide her through, especially to encourage her own softness toward Farah and to see Farah's qualities as positive. I tried to help her interrupt the pattern of harsh parenting that she had experienced as a child and which she was perpetuating with her children.

Much of what I did with Farah in individual sessions was to create an artistic environment, to establish a quiet, aesthetic oasis where Farah could feel safe and free. Farah was excited by the art materials in my workspace. She thoroughly enjoyed making things and always planned her sessions from one to the next. She was orderly and very precise, with a tendency to perfectionism. Sometimes this tendency would interfere with her enjoyment of the process.

Her beginning productions were rather stiff and formal, typical paintings of a school-child variety—clearly defined earth and sky with a rather barren or agitated scene in the middle space. One of her paintings from the beginning phase of therapy was quite striking and important and unlike these more typical works. She painted a girl who was angry and had a "mess in her tummy." We discussed the girl and what she might be angry about, trying to generate a story around her. In my mind, of course, I was thinking that this was Farah. However, the closer that I got to a story like Farah's, the more she wanted to leave this image and pass on to less emotional or personal subjects.

What became her signature works and the focus of tremendous time and energy were a series of clay containers which she fired and glazed. The containers included bowls, baskets, mugs, and cups. Some were open vessels and others had lids. This transition from the angry girl to the containers was an interesting one. On the one hand, I understood the move as an attempt to deal with the anxiety that was aroused by the image of her rage put so starkly and so bluntly. Farah was a subtle and outwardly a sweet and ultra-cooperative patient. My sense was that she had let me see this angry part of her and was quite shocked at its appearance. There was, I think, an opposition being expressed here in terms of the duality of her inner experience. Both rage and containment were operating within Farah.

This dual experience was not only Farah's internal experience and the source of tremendous conflict for her, it was also played out in her mother's inner world and, most significantly, in the clash between cultures experienced by the family which had emigrated from a Muslim country. Mrs. B. was certainly angry or depressed almost all of the time. She had high hopes and ambitions for her daughters to be successful in Canadian culture. She herself was highly driven and ambitious. She was buying and selling houses with very little money on hand, trying to work and make it. She hardly slept and was in a fairly constant state of worry and anxiety. Set against this driving ambition to be successful was her fundamentalist Muslim religious belief.

This aspect of family life became a significant element in my work with Farah and with Mrs. B. It was also part of the dynamic emerging around the conflict between rage and containment embodied in Farah's artistic imagery. Mrs. B. belonged to a Muslim community; her life revolved around the activities at the Mosque. The family was highly observant, and both Mrs. B. and the children wore the traditional Muslim headscarf (hejab) for women. Often, however, Mrs. B. would remove the hejab in sessions with me, especially when more emotional material was surfacing. Farah often came for her sessions without the hejab, associating our work together as different from the confinement of the hejab. I have long hair, and Farah would comment on it, noticing when I wore it free-flowing and when I tied it back in various ways. She liked the free-flowing style, even though her own hair was tied back all of the time. My sense was that the wearing of the hejab and the exposed head were also an embodiment of this conflict between open expression of feeling and containment.

As I worked with Farah and met periodically with Mrs. B., either alone or in joint sessions with Farah, the clash between cultures became more and more apparent. At times, it created an interesting and lively juxtaposition for our work. Mrs. B. could argue with me about child-rearing practices in Canada vs. her own country; Farah could see clearly the opposition between our open work and her strict and routinized home experience of many chores and religious observance. Many times, however, it was frustrating and painful for all of us. It created a conflict for Farah where she began to wish she were my daughter, desiring to be free of the restrictions imposed by her mother and her religion. For Mrs. B., although she appreciated my caring presence in their lives and called me often in distress and confusion, I slowly became associated with her daughter's rebelliousness and anger toward her.

If I encouraged Farah to express her feelings, as all therapy must do, then Farah was considered bad at home. According to Mrs. B., the Koran dictates that children, especially female children, must be quiet, respectful of their parents, never speak up, and generally submit to the will of their elders. Mrs. B.'s own conflict between wanting success in the North American sense and the dictates of her religion and culture was overwhelming; I think she often played this out in her relationship with me. I became the Jewish/North American/Woman/Feminist/Artist who was luring her daughter to another world and ultimately away from the family.

Tensions were heightened when a marriage was arranged by the Muslim community for Mrs. B. The entrance of a man into the home created further anxiety for Mrs. B. in relation to her daughters. Now containment was crucial in terms, particularly, of their sexuality. Mrs. B. became, over time, quite concerned about Farah and her step-father becoming sexually involved. Her mother expressed her fears quite openly and dramatically; Farah, a very modest and basically shy girl, was mortified. Her mother aggressively pursued these fearful fantasies, not allowing Farah ever to be alone with her step-father. Two things were operating here for Farah: one was her feeling that her step-father was a kind and gentle man with whom she found a softness and almost maternal presence, the other was anger with her mother often played out by being openly physical with her step-father in her mother's presence.

The birth of a new child, a boy, brought some mitigation to the situation. Mrs. B. now had a consuming focus away from Farah which helped reduce tensions for awhile. But not long after the first few months, Mrs. B. was feeling anxious about money—her new husband, recently in the country, had no legal status and could only find menial work. As well, Mrs. B. left the baby in the care of her daughters. From Mrs. B's point of view, Hala was the "perfect little mother" for Mohammed, while Farah was "only interested in playing with him." My attempts to point out the importance of play for the baby's development seemed to fall on deaf ears. It was always difficult to know whether anything I said had any impact on Mrs. B. and her thoughts or actions.

Throughout this period of perpetual turmoil and distress at home, Farah continued to come faithfully to her therapy sessions and to make the clay containers, some of which she left with me and others she gave to her mother, almost like peace offerings. She made some useful household objects such as a spoon rest for cooking. As with other objects that she brought home, she often told of how they were damaged or broken there. She told these stories with a kind of resignation. At one point during this period, Farah came to therapy with a clay cat that she had made at school but that had gotten distorted in the kiln upon firing. She wanted to recreate this cat image with me and to get it right. To me, the end product resembled a snake coiled to attack, rather than a cat. Certainly, in terms of an image of controlled energy, the cat was striking.

I introduced at this time a blank journal book to Farah. In the book, she kept stories that she told, inventories of her favorite colors and activities, and drawings. The book became an important repository for Farah, and she came back to it in each session. She especially wanted to keep the book as a private document, only sharing it with me and not with her mother. There was, increasingly, the sense that the world of the therapy space and the world at home were growing further and further apart. I felt that this was unfortunate but necessary in order to work with Farah and to support her in recognizing all of her feelings. Less and less did Mrs. B. come for joint sessions, partially because of the demands of her new baby and also because the family had moved quite a long distance away from the agency.

It was the arrival of Farah's natural father with his family that brought about the termination of therapy with Farah. At this point, I had been involved with the family for almost three years and, despite ongoing differences and tensions between us, Mrs. B. still felt that therapy was important for Farah. Somewhere inside of her, Mrs. B. recognized Farah's need for a psychic oasis and a space where she could be accepted and appreciated. I always felt that one source of Mrs. B.'s rage toward Farah and, at times, toward me had to do with her envy of the therapy space. Once when she came with Farah, mother and daughter made clay containters together and even glazed them in a subsequent session. Mrs. B. thoroughly enjoyed herself, especially the feeling of the wet clay on her hands. She seemed happier than I had ever seen her that day, taking much pride in what she had created. Unfortunately, sustaining this creative energy was almost impossible for Mrs. B.

With Mr. B.'s return, many old memories and feelings began to surface for Mrs. B. She was aware of her tendency to take out her anger on Farah but unwilling to go for therapy for herself, something that I had attempted to set up for her many times in the past. In addition, Mrs. B.'s relationship to her new husband was floundering. At first, they had been attracted to each other but, after two years and the birth of a child, there were significant strains emerging. Mr. A.'s status in Canada was still unresolved; he had not told his family back home about his marriage (since Mrs. B. was a divorcee with two children, it would not have been an acceptable marriage from the point of view of his culture); and, from Mrs. B.'s report, he was unwilling to be a co-parent with her around her daughters. For Farah as well, her father's return was bringing memories to the surface. She remembered being beaten in his sister's house and his general neglect of her. She was angry at her father and her mother at this point, disappointed in her step-father and feeling that I was the only adult with whom she could communicate.

In the midst of this turmoil, Mrs. B. insisted that Farah take on a job after school to help support the family. This job, cashier in a market, began to interfere with coming for therapy. One day Farah arrived for her appointment an hour early and came in quite upset and agitated. She was not at all happy with the after-school job; and her mother was threatening that if she did not stay with it, she would send her to live with her father. Farah felt as if she could not live anywhere; she felt trapped.

The day after this session, Mrs. B. called me to inform me that Farah would no longer be attending sessions with me. She said that her ex-husband, her current husband and herself agreed that I had been "poisoning Farah's mind," that Muslim culture demands that girls obey their parents and that this kind of up-bringing is a rehearsal for girls to obey their husbands. When Farah had complained to me of her sense that neither parent wanted her, we had spoken about the idea of a foster home. Mrs. B. was furious with me for having discussed this idea with Farah and, on this basis, was cutting off contact with me.

This agitated termination occurred in the late fall of 1990. Art-making had been severly curtailed throughout the period of unrest regarding Farah's living situation. The only thing that Farah had with her was her journal book which she had taken home prior to the sudden cut-off from me. I received periodic phone calls from Farah and from Mrs. B. in the next few months. Once, Farah called me in "dire emergency" wanting to discuss the idea of a foster home. Several months later, Mrs. B. called to complain about Farah, saying that if she lived in a Muslim country, she would "beat some sense into her." Mrs. B. asked that I talk to Farah to "straighten her out." At this point, I recommended a Muslim psychiatrist for Mrs. B., and she began seeing him.

Although I had closed the case formally at the agency, Mrs. B. called in the fall of 1991 to request therapy again for Farah. In negotiating with Mrs. B. and with Farah, it was clear that some of their more acute problems had really never been successfully addressed: Farah was still quite angry and rebellious, Mrs. B. was still profoundly depressed, and there was still a fundamental lack of differentiation between mother and daughter. Mrs. B. continued, as she always had, to blame Farah for all the difficulties in the family. Also, Mrs. B. was requesting at this point that Farah's resumption of therapy be kept secret from her step-father, lest he disagree and become angry with the decision to resume. I refused to see Farah unless the step-father was aware of the therapy. I was concerned that seeing Farah behind his back would continue to foster the splitting and the secrecy that was already so prominent in this family system.

Ultimately, Mrs. B. refused to tell him; and, although she desperately needed the support, Farah could not see me.

In early June of 1993, after hearing almost nothing from the family, Mrs. B. called me from a hospital in Toronto to tell me that she was in the process of undergoing treatments for cancer. She was extremely ill and had contacted me because she feared that she might die. She wanted me to become involved again with Farah. Although I was leaving soon for the summer, I visited Mrs. B. in the hospital as well as spoke to Farah several times by phone.

In a curious way, Farah, sixteen years old at this point, was relieved that she could finally talk to me openly with her mother's approval and that her mother was not home now so that things were more peaceful there. Mrs. B. had made some earlier arrangements for Farah to be married to a young man, and now she felt a pressing need to organize this marriage as quickly as possible. Farah spoke to me about her ambivalence regarding the marriage. She felt that, in many ways, this might be her only hope of getting free of her mother and leaving her mother's house. She had thought about living with her father but rejected it because of her anger at him over the past. She hoped that this man would be someone who would approve of her continuing her education. She wanted to go to university and not to have children right away.

In our discussions, the issue of the marriage was helping to clarify for her what she wanted in her life. I even began to feel that the marriage might be appropriate for Farah, given the demands of her culture. Farah noted that she would be able at any point to veto the arrangement if, after meeting the man, she did not like him. The only hesitation even initally was the fact that this man was quite religious and related to a strict Muslim family in their community; therefore, it would be expected that Farah would observe Muslim practices strictly. Farah, at this point in time, was questioning her culture and, especially, its attitudes toward women. She was not saying her prayers as regularly, which was a big departure for her.

After the summer, in the fall of 1993 and into the winter and spring of 1994, I had a regularly scheduled phone contact with Farah. Mrs. B. recovered and the cancer went into remission. My contact during this period was with Farah exclusively. She would call me from a phone at school since her mother was home and functioning again and had forbidden Farah to speak to me.

Farah had used the journal book faithfully throughout the period from the sudden termination of treatment in the fall of 1990 to the present. She has told me that the book is a representation of me and of our relationship. When she writes in the book, it is as if she is talking to me. In anticipation of our weekly talk, Farah organizes the topics. In one of the early calls, Farah's topics included: marriage, living at home, religion, and thoughts about suicide. These calls were significant for Farah because she literally had no one to speak to about these important concerns. She had been feeling suicidal off and on during this period. A book which she read about teenage suicide from the school library was helpful in naming the feelings that she experienced. Writing in the journal also seemed to mitigate these feelings. The journal work conjured up, for her, a transitional object with which she could feel connected. This transitional object told her that she was creative and sensitive and helped to form a buffer between herself and her mother who had become a bad and punishing figure for her.

Things at home were still highly conflictual. Farah reported spending much time in her room crying. Our discussions centered around ways that Farah could distance herself emotionally from her mother's intense dramas and not get caught up with her so much. Farah also seemed to be flooded with memories about her four years at her father's house. She shared with me memories of being beaten, locked in her room for whole days at a time, and other fairly detailed memories of abusive situations about which she was too afraid to tell anyone else.

In one of our last conversations before my summer break, we spent an extended time talking about art. This was the first time that we had returned to the subject in many years. Farah began asking me what my paintings were like. I asked her, in good therapist fashion, to tell me what she imagined she saw in her mind about my paintings. Immediately Farah said that they were abstract paintings with bright colors, and that maybe they looked like landscapes. Farah had obviously remembered some of the painting that we had done together so many years before and held my style in her mind. Farah told me that she had been making jugs and vases, painting them with flower patterns. It was interesting to me that after all this time, art-making was still an important activity for Farah and functioned to help her define herself.

Farah is still making containers, still working on the containment of her inner world and struggling with the rage and conflict that swirls around her. Containers are not constricting for Farah. As opposed to the strict dogmatic stance of her fundamentalist beliefs, which Farah has experienced as so constricting, the containers hold gently. These containers are beautiful vessels of soul and spirit. The flower patterns seem appropriate in terms of the metaphor or image that I carry about Farah: the delicate flower, opening and discovering a world full of pain and confusion and struggling not to close completely in response. The making of containers and their decoration helps Farah to create a quiet aesthetic oasis for herself and shows that beauty is an important source of solace for her.

The journal book, the telephone, and the creation of a speech-space are her ways of keeping the connection to me which have helped Farah survive in a difficult situation. They are all transitional objects. In many ways, I think that her imagination has saved her. It was the vividness of her imaginal world that impressed the initial assessors at the agency. Farah entered the world with a strong will to survive and a deep need to express herself. I feel that Farah's case illustrates well the sense of primary creativity that I am exploring in this book. Farah's creativity was not met adequately in her relationship with her mother, and yet she retained this aliveness throughout her life. The therapeutic relationship was powerful for her because it provided a good environment for mirroring her creativity. It was this strong capacity for the creation of an imaginal, transitional space that I helped to foster in Farah and that perhaps will help to carry her forward into her adult life.

Creativity: Reality or Phantasy?

Angela came to see me for individual therapy in March of 1990, when she was almost twelve years old. She was referred because her mother, who was seeing another therapist at the agency, was experiencing more and more difficulty with her. She was fighting at home and at school, moody, rude, and defiant. Although Mrs. D., her mother, was not thrilled about the idea of therapy for her daughter, she was desperately seeking solutions to the problems at home and at school. Angela lived in a very dangerous and poor downtown neighborhood. Both of her parents were involved with drugs at various times. Angela had two brothers—one older by two years and one younger by five years. All the children had the same father. He visited them occasionally but not regularly. Mrs. D. came from a violent and abusive background. The fact that her mother was white and her father black figured prominently in Angela's view of herself. She often referred to herself as a "half-breed" and was only interested in white boys.

Angela fell asleep in the waiting room of the agency before her first appointment with me. I had to wake her up in order to bring her upstairs. She said that she had been very tired—I wondered about how much sleep she was getting at home. Despite the way in which Angela had been described by her mother, I found her to be initially quiet, shy, and compliant. In fact, in the first session, I felt that I had to be quite directive in order to engage with her. We did a mutual drawing as our first work: a girl in the rain at the playground, getting wet. In my drawing turns, I offered her an umbrella and an apple tree for shelter. I noted (to myself) that Angela's girl looked rather helpless (no arms or real hands), powerless, and alone. We also wrote poetry together where I gave Angela a stack of words to choose from randomly and construct a poem.

The poem read as follows (her chosen words are italicized):

Her *claws* made *blood*
and the *wind* blew
she crossed the *bridge*
and made a *home* in the *grass*

Angela was pleased with the poem; it was done with ease and enjoyment. As we did the mutual art-making and the session progressed, I could feel Angela's energy increase. I had the sense that I was beginning to convey to her that her work would be acceptable in my space. At the end of the session, Angela offered to bring her artwork from school to show me and told me that she wanted to draw another picture together next time.

Angela came back the next week eager to get started. She was incredibly talkative and was already feeling that our sessions were helping her to improve at school. She said that she was learning to control her temper and ignore the kids who bugged her. She wanted to draw another picture together and write a story about it as we did last time. The story about the picture was as follows: Angela and I are on an island in the middle of the sea. We sailed together in a big boat, away from Toronto and the city, from the cars, the pollution, the noise, the dirt; and when we got to the open sea, the sky was clear. There were birds everywhere, and we saw beautiful fish swimming in the sea. The sea was blue and clear. A boat passed by, and we heard music. We waved hello to the boat filled with music, and it started to come to visit us.

For me, this lush fantasy embodied the way in which Angela was already experiencing the therapeutic/artistic space. I also contributed my images to the scene, as if inviting her to be with me in this rich place. In a sense, the story has the same theme as the poem: the need to get away completely from all the bad things, the wish for a place of beauty and sanctuary, true home. At the end of this session, Angela wrote me a note: " To Ellen—thank you for helping me know you better and feel better. I really feel better now because now I think I can draw better than last week. Thank you very much. Angela" This wishing was a strong force in Angela's character. On the one hand, it was gratifying to me to be considered already so important in her life. On the other hand, I was aware that this was happening too soon.

I wondered if Angela's need was so great that she tended to fantasize the existence of an idealized relationship even before she had a chance to allow herself to experience its reality. The danger, of course, in allowing a real relationship to unfold over time is that one can be disappointed. Angela had, many times, been disappointed by caregivers. Her father was extremely inconsistent and her mother, at times, either too depressed, too angry, or too preoccupied to care for her adequately. She had seen many adults in her environment succumb to drugs, prostitution, and criminal activity. How could she know that I would be different?

In the following sessions, Angela continued to be eager and hungry for what she was getting from our relationship. She demonstrated this engagement by bringing things of interest to her into the sessions. Many times she brought tapes which she wanted to hear and to play for me. The tapes in this early period were by The New Kids on the Block, her current obsession. She fantasized that if Jordan from the New Kids would come to her house, then her behaviour would change. She also spoke about the lack of attention at home and about her father and how much she missed him. Angela played the tapes for me, was able to sing all the songs by heart and showed me her dance moves to accompany the songs.

While I felt that I was getting a glimpse into Angela's world, I also felt that she was holding me at a distance, not wanting to get too close. With this feeling in mind, I introduced the idea of our using the tape recorder not just to listen to her music, but to create our own tapes. Angela liked this idea and immediately thought of interviewing me. In this format, she was able to ask questions about me and satisfy some of her curiosity about who I was—i.e., do you like your work? Are you married? Do you have children? These kind of questions are typical in the initial phases of work with children who need to get a sense of the real person behind the role as well as explore and name the transference fantasies that are aroused in the relationship.

What is interesting in expressive arts therapy work is that we can create a form for this experience to take place which is neither real nor un-real but exists in a play-space which is in-between and thereby protected and safe. The creation of the frame of the interview provided a container for approaching intimacy which would normally be quite threatening if expressed directly. The interview gave Angela permission to gain access to me at a distance and playfully. She became an Oprah Winfrey character, playing her role with a lot of style and humour.   This allowed her to be freer, even utterly outrageous at times, and to lose some of her wariness of me.

Out of the interview idea came another creative structure: Angela and I made up a rap song together which we recorded. This song was called, "We're the B Girls":

> Hi, I'm Angela and this is Ellen
> We're the B Girls and we're yellin
> You mess with the best
> And you die like the rest
> We're trying to tell you that we're the tops
> And if you don't believe us just go to the cops
> And if the cops don't come
> Just cry to your mom
>
> We're the B Girls
> Just look at our curls
> We're the B Girls
> Just look at our curls
> We're the B B B B B B Girls
> We're the B B B B B B Girls
>
> Take a look at us
> You must
> Take a look at us
> You must

If we make you sick
Then run very quick
Home
Write a poem
Then take a chill
Then call Bill and he'll ill

We're the B B B B B B Girls
We're the B B B B B B Girls!!!!

We would return to this song again and again throughout the first few months of therapy. It often acted as a reminder of the us-ness of our relationship and created a kind of cement between us. As the summer of 1990 and the close of our sessions until September drew near, Angela initiated a kind of play that became extremely important as therapy proceeded. It was the custom for Angela to come for her session with me directly after her session with her mother and siblings. Sometimes she was quiet and withdrawn after these meetings but, at other times, she would arrive in a mood to get down to work with me and might share some of the discussion from the family session. In this particular session near the end of June, Angela spoke about her mother's boyfriend who had been living with the family and how much she disliked him. She said that he seemed to create a lot of fights with her older brother and added to the chaos at home. Angela made up a game in which I was the mother and she was the daughter. I was easy-going, and her Dad was strict. We lived apart. In the game, the building where they lived was very dangerous, and the daughter would listen to music as a way of protecting herself from the dangers. Although this was a dramatic enactment, it did not depart in crucial respects from the actual drama of Angela's life experience. It gave me a feel for what Angela went through daily and how she managed to cope with her lfe.

It seemed clear from her use of the arts in the therapy space that artistic activity was oxygen and calcium for Angela, essential to her survival in a rough and hostile world. I had a hard time imagining what life would be like for her without music, dance, drama, poetry and the whole realm of the imaginal.

Music, especially, seemed to create another world into which Angela could move in order to find some solace. The lyrics of songs were important to her, especially songs about love gone wrong. Many times she would pretend to be the singer of one of these very romantic songs and lip-synch the words. Her whole body would be engaged in these experiences; she was one with the song, the music, and the emotion.

In the fall, Angela began to write her own songs in our sessions:

The Beach

> I was walking on the beach
> and you were beside me
> I saw your shadow
> coming toward me
> You frighten me
> I jumped and I looked at you
> You smiled   I smiled
>
> We were walking home
> and we saw firecrackers
> popping in the sky
>
> We went home
> Got our firecrackers
> And came back to the park
>
> And started to do them
> We did them all
> Then went to the beach
> and had a picnic
>
> It was 12:00
> and we went home
> and we kissed goodbye
> You went to your house

I thought to myself
what a wonderful day this has been.

UNTITLED (after Suzanne Vega)

I was sitting in the kitchen and
waiting for my coffee

When along came my friend and
asked me to go swimming

I didn't feel like going so
she got all upset
So she screamed and got angry
and left me with my father

So I got up and in anger
I ran up to the bathroom

My father came to find me
and was banging on the door

I opened up the door and slipped
on past my father

He called out my name
and I just kept on walking

So he left our house and
I was still crying

I wish my father cared
when I got upset.

Angela dictated both of these songs to me and was careful
to make sure that I wrote them down according to her specifi-
cations. Obviously, from the themes in her material one got

the sense of a girl who deeply longed for connection, although relationships were fraught with fear and with conflict.

In January of 1991, Angela brought a story that she had written at school and for which she received a great deal of praise from her teachers.

A Tall Tale

Once upon a time, there lived a girl named Angela. She had three step-sisters named Crystal, Jennifer and Shelly and the step-mother's name was Mrs. Newman. She had strict rules. They had to clean every single day. They had to wash dishes everyday after dinner. They couldn't take a rest. They were so tired. They did not go to school. Every morning they had to wake up at 6:30 to start cleaning. They only had a little time to sleep. Angela had to clean the most of all. Jennifer and Shelly were allowed to have boyfriends but not Angela. She was so jealous. But only one friend of Angela's was allowed in.   Her friend Janelle was so afraid of Mrs. Newman. She always yelled at Janelle. Angela asked if she could go outside. Mrs. Newman said yes but only for one hour. She said "Oh! No!" So they went outside and Angela ran away because she didn't want to live with Janelle. It was past one hour and Mrs. Newman came looking for her. The first place she went was the police station. Then she went to her real Dad's house, Angela's real Dad. She wasn't there. So she went to Janelle's. So Janelle came to the door and said that she wasn't there. But she really was. Janelle said "She just left."   So Mrs. Newman said "Thank you and goodbye." Janelle shut the door and Angela said "Thank you, Janelle, I am really so happy that I don't have to go back to that house every again." So Angela went to her Dad's house and they lived happily ever after.

P.S. Mrs. Newman never found Angela

The End

The unfairness of life, being singled out for preferential treat-ment, and the wish to be rescued and to live somewhere else, the Cinderella motif, seem to be Angela's story. The only op-tion is to run away. This is the case in the story; but in Angela's real life, she does little running. Mrs. D. usually knows where Angela is if she is outside of the house. Her means of getting away is to go deeply into her songs and to withdraw into her own world. I was certainly glad that Angela was able to bring that aspect of herself into therapy and share it with me.

From January to mid-April, however, it began to feel as though sharing the songs with me was becoming uninteresting to her and to me, almost an excuse for not engaging with me or with herself. Angela missed many sessions during this pe-riod, partly due to school trips and holidays when she claimed she forgot to come. The missed sessions and the repetitive na-ture of the sessions that we did have began to make me feel bored and disconnected from her. I am always interested in using my own feelings as a barometer of what might be going on in the relationship. I felt strongly at this point that for Angela to succeed in distancing herself from me and from therapy would work against her being able to get the help that she needed so much. At almost the same time that I was feeling this lack of connection, Angela forgot to bring tapes to her session and in-troduced again the idea, dormant for several months, of doing an interview with me. The interview began with her playing the role of her current boyfriend, Ryan, and me trying to find out more about him. The interview format quickly developed into a drama about me as a little girl. Angela played the role of the mother who is a witch-like figure. The mother kills the fa-ther and tries to stab and kill the girl (me). The mother keeps going out and leaving the girl at home alone. When she re-turns, she is drunk and very menacing. Without warning, mother turns over a new leaf. She remarries her first husband (my fa-ther) who gives her a lot of money.   I also discover that I have a long-lost sister. The mother and the sister are pregnant.

In another session at this time, the scenario involved a mother who was a hooker, who chain-smoked and got drunk. She neglected her daughter, continually abandoning her. One time a robber, also played by Angela, entered and raped the girl (me) at gunpoint. Her mother was so drunk that she had a heart attack. The girl saved her mother by calling an ambulance. The mother, however, was angry all of the time, and the girl threatened to take the mother to court for her behaviour. The mother, again, was pregnant and also accused the girl of being pregnant.

These dramatic enactments became more and more compelling for Angela. In May and June of 1991, Angela would enter the room and immediately begin the enactment where we had left off the last time. These enactments continued to have the same structure: a sadistic, cruel, punishing and unpredictable mother, men who were kidnappers or rapists, and the daughter figure who was a helpless victim. The play often involved using baby dolls who, like the daughter, were helpless victims. The theme of babies and pregnancy was dominant for quite awhile. In one session, Angela brought her own baby doll from home to be incorporated into the scenario: I, as the daughter, had a baby and my mother (Angela) did not know about it. My boyfriend (also played by Angela) was no good and tried to kill the baby. The mother kept flipping from good to bad. Many times the mother, in her good appearance, fell asleep holding the baby in a kind of cozy, close embrace of mutual relaxation. This suddenly and without warning changed into the mother as persecutor, hurting the daughter, the baby, and herself. The daughter tried to take revenge on the mother, but the mother is superhuman and does not die no matter what the daughter does.

On several occasions, Angela would find it quite difficult to come out of these dramas and would be unable to make a distinction between the fantasy world of the drama and the reality of being at the agency. At these times, I needed to give her time to de-brief before leaving. Here we can see the work with fire in action. The question was how much to try to structure the situations and how much to just let the fire burn almost to the point of wildness. I kept trusting, however, that the container of the transitional space in the form of the drama would carry the fire and provide safety.

In early May of 1991, I attended a school meeting in which the teachers were reviewing Angela's progress and planning for her for next year. There was a general sense that Angela had made quite significant improvements in school during the last year. The school personnel seemed to like Angela and had a supportive attitude toward her. They felt that she was extremely bonded to the school and could see that she was beginning to react strongly to moving on to her next school placement. There was a recommendation that she be integrated into a regular classroom at her new school. For Angela, who had tended to be placed in "behavioural classes," this was a very good sign.

The dramas that Angela continued to create and enact in therapy grew more and more violent. It was appropriate that Angela bring all her pain, fear, aggression, and sadism into therapy sessions and have the opportunity to have a witness for all of the mess in her life. It was encouraging at this point to hear that school was going well and that teachers would understand her reactions to leaving the school and not be threatened by her sometimes negative behaviour. I was, however, unclear about what was going on at home. Mrs. D. was not attending regular appointments with me and had stopped seeing her therapist at the agency. She was not communicating with the school as she regularly did. There were rumors that she was dealing cocaine from her apartment and had sold much of their furniture, the t.v., etc., to buy drugs. I continued to be concerned for Angela's safety at home, but she was not saying anything directly to me. Angela had experience with the authorities, and the Children's Aid Society had been involved with her family before. She was definitely scared to betray her mother in this respect. Because I had no concrete evidence of danger, I could not do anything about it.

I felt quite sure that the content of the dramas was indicative of the kind of world in which Angela lived. But was there a one-to-one correspondence between Angela's experience and her imaginative representation of it in these enactments? How much was real and how much was fantasy? How much was a reflection of an internal state of confusion and terror, longing and desire, and how much was directly taken from her external life?

I found myself fascinated, horrified, afraid, angry, amazed, and quite concerned about this material. Angela's unflinching way of enacting all this horror was impressive. I trusted that she felt safe. I sometimes had to protect the space and us by breaking out of the drama and reminding Angela that she was in the room with me and that she needed to be careful. With all of my child patients, the only rule in therapy is that we cannot hurt each other. Sometimes I had to remind Angela of that rule because she would get so carried away. Perhaps for Angela the question of reality or fantasy was irrelevant. This play was truly essential work for her and desperately needed to go on. I never felt so frightened that I felt the play needed to be stopped. I felt that the more I could tolerate and allow, the better it would be for Angela.

As we moved toward the break for summer holidays, Angela began looking forward to her graduation ceremony and invited me to attend. She began bringing tapes and food to the sessions and introduced some new material to the dramas: now I am the daughter and my babies have been placed in foster care. The babies are being returned from care but my mother (Angela) is fighting to take my babies away. She is evil. There are social workers and policemen involved now (mitigating forces, almost for the first time), but no one can deal with my mother who is, like before, superhuman and incapable of being killed.

In the last session before the summer, there was a noticeable shift in the play. The week before, the daughter had run away and was placed in a foster home where the family was rich. In this scenario, the mother had discovered the daughter and had gone to take her back. In the last session, on the other hand, the mother had finally died and the daughter was placed by a social worker in a foster home. The foster parents were very wealthy. There was plenty of food and the foster mother was the kind of mother who did everything for the daughter but who was away working a lot. She allowed the daughter to have boys over for pizza and dancing parties. The daughter (played by me) and her friend (played by Angela) talked about clothes, about wearing sexy clothes on the street and attracting attention from men and from boys. I wondered if my leaving had anything to do with the reshaping of the material at this point. Perhaps Angela was anticipating the loss of someone with whom she could engage and who was supportive to her.

In September, Angela returned for therapy, eager and excited to be back. She had had a difficult summer—she had gotten kicked out of camp for threatening a counselor and another camper and told me she had been "molested" at a relative's house by a man who "touched my breasts." Angela was very scared by this experience and also expressed reluctance to attend her new school. Themes of sex and pregnancy dominated her scenarios in the fall, with the dominant characters being two sisters who band together and conspire to leave our bad parents who are impossible. The older sister, played by Angela, is very maternal toward her younger sister. She talks to her about boys, warning her not to have sex too young, to do her homework, and to stay in school. But the younger sister is wild and won't listen to her sister. She gets pregnant and goes to Jamaica to have the baby.

In her real life, Angela was skipping school at this time and afraid to sleep at home. Mrs. D. was embroiled in a violent confrontation with a man who kept coming to their apartment in the middle of the night and banging on the door. Angela said she was extremely scared by this. Angela, in this mid-October session, had come with a drama already formulated: She plays Carol, a crackhead, who gets me (Michelle, the younger sister in the other dramas) involved with drugs. Michelle dies of an overdose. Carol comes over and harasses Tracy (the older, wiser sister). Carol's boyfriend, who is a "psycho," tries to rape and murder Tracy and her children. Angela put a great deal of energy in playing the character of the boyfriend. I began making some links in this session between the character of the boyfriend in the drama and the man who was harassing Angela's family at home. This seemed to be helpful to Angela.

From this point in late October of 1991, things with Angela began to slide downward. She was not attending school regularly and began to come less and less often for therapy sessions. When she did come to see me, she seemed listless, tired and uninvolved. I felt like I was losing her in some deep and fundamental way. Mrs. D. did not show up for several appointments that we made nor did she answer the telephone very often. Many times when I called, a strange voice would answer and say that everyone was asleep. At this time, I had more contact with her teachers at school and with the Children's Aid Society (CAS) worker than I did with Angela. Her teacher reported significant problems with Angela at school: skipping classes, temper outbursts, leaving the building without permission, and simply not showing up on most days. The CAS worker kept visiting the home and claiming that, while the apartment was practically bare, she never saw any dangerous or criminal activity actually going on. She was pressuring Angela with a threat that if she did not go to school or see me regularly, she would be placed in care. In March of 1992, the worker had a feeling that Angela was pregnant. This ultimately proved to be a false rumor.

While I kept the hour open for Angela, she did not show up or call me for several months. In the beginning of April, 1992, I spoke to one of her teachers at school who said that she had begun coming to school again. The teacher told me that Angela had two court dates pending: one where she was a witness to a sexual assault and the other where she had been charged with mischief over $1000.00. In the latter situation, Angela had broken a local storeowner's window in anger because he, apparently, had called her a "slut."

On this same day, Angela showed up for her regular appointment time. She was ready to begin again as if no time had passed. We listened to some old interview and song tapes that we had made together and then a drama emerged: we are two sisters. Angela is the older sister who is trying to get me to shape up and go to school. The older sister talked to me about how it was when she was my age and all the mistakes that she made. Angela was extremely tired on this day, and, after the dramatic enactment, she lay down and talked to me about some of the things that had been going on recently. She was keeping very late hours, getting drunk, and her mother had gotten seriously beaten up. We talked about things getting out of control lately. Angela seemed very comfortable in the space and, in the last fifteen minutes of the session, she fell asleep. When I woke her, she seemed quite confused and disoriented.

The next time that I heard about Angela, in May of 1992, was from the CAS worker who told me that Angela had been arrested on drug charges (selling cocaine) and was placed in a group home outside of the city. Apparently, she was not doing too well there. She had run away several times. In October of 1992, I received a letter from Angela. In the letter, which was written in a rather breezy tone, Angela told me about the group home, about her boyfriend who was in jail at the time, and some of her feelings about sex.

I wrote back to Angela but heard nothing from this time (October) until late March of 1994. Angela was back in the city at this point and had been in two different group homes for a year and a half. She called me and we scheduled an appointment. In the session, she seemed a bit unclear about her plans although I did feel a strong desire on her part to reconnect. She was interested in the fact that my space looked just the same as before. The session was brief and involved a bit of catching up and planning for future sessions. This was the last time that I saw Angela.

In reflecting upon my work with Angela, I am struck by the way in which her real life and her fantasy or imaginal life interconnected and interpenetrated. There was no doubt that Angela loved expressing herself in artistic forms: music, dance, poetry and drama were all familiar and comfortable for her. But her expression went beyond simple enjoyment. For her, this was essential activity, as important as sleeping and eating. The more frantic and chaotic her life became during the course of our work, the more I felt her urgency in putting all the anxiety and terror into a form for herself.

The form was close to real life but not an exact replication of it. It differed in significant ways. First, there was the importance of the witness. My presence in terms of holding the space consistently for her and being involved in the dramas, mostly as a partner or a self-representation, was crucial for Angela. She could take things all the way, knowing that I could make it safe for her. Secondly, the self-representation was interesting: I was a young, naive, and impressionable character, an innocent. This was, of course, an important part of Angela that needed expression. Very often the self that she presented to the world was tough and aggressive. She needed to act like the young child that she was, and this aspect of her needed to be embodied in the form of a role once removed from herself. For me to play the role also indicated that this part would be recognized by someone. Thirdly, in the dramas Angela could experiment with scenarios that went way beyond the limits of reality. As bad as her real life was, she could explore the vast reaches of her imagination in terms of violence, of pregnancy and babies, of cruel men and incredibly arbitrary and inconsistent mothers. The question of the drama was always *what if* things got this bad, *what could happen?* The experimentation could also go in the other direction: what would happen if there was an older sister who could partner with me and guide me, or a good mother in my life?

Ultimately, however, the major obstacle to Angela's use of her imagination was, of course, the real situation of her life. When reality became too overwhelming, it overrode her imagination and created too much anxiety for her to be able to transform it through art. What I am suggesting here is that there may be a necessary amount of pain for creativity to take place; but the psyche can become overloaded and, then, the imagination is short-circuited. As much as Angela needed and craved the creative source, her life simply did not permit her to tap into it at times. When I look over our work together, it seems that there was a period of improvement for Angela which coincided with home being relatively calm and predictable and school being extremely supportive. With these two variables in place, Angela could relax into the sessions and use what the transitional space could offer her. As expressive arts therapists, we cannot underestimate the power of the real as it creates the context for our work. We can address it as much as possible, but we need to recognize when it interferes with the work that we are trying to do.

Like Farah, the imaginal was a crucial, essential bodily need for Angela. Although I am sure that Farah will continue to pursue art-making, I cannot be so sure about Angela. I expect her to reappear at the agency again at some point. The thread, while thin right now, is still connecting me to her. I have written to her. My regret is that I am not able at the moment to provide a space and the witness for her. My hope is that, holding on to the memory of our work together, she will be able at some point to find a creative space again.

Creativity: Collective Co-Imagining

Three years ago, I approached the residential unit of the agency where I work with a proposal to begin an arts therapy group with the adolescents. There is a self-contained, 16 bed in-patient unit on the top floor of the agency. Adolescents live there and attend a school program on the premises. Stays range from a few months to three years in some cases. In the past, I had tried to start an out-patient group for teens but had not been successful; and I felt that, since the participants would be readily available, the unit was an ideal source. There was some discussion amongst the staff about the advisability of a group within the unit as special and set apart. Some staff felt that since the treatment in general focuses upon the concept of the milieu, it would not be a good idea to single some people out. Other staff could see that a group focusing on artistic expression would be a unique complement to the services provided. There was an adolescent interpersonal group that had been going on for some time, and the focus of this group was discussion. Staff could see that some of the kids were not able to function in a purely verbal group, and they needed to express themselves in less linear modes.

After the group was constituted, we developed a structure and a routine for our activities. We began each group with a check-in where each member talked about their week and expressed their readiness or not-readiness to begin the group. Since all of the teens lived together, there were few surprises about what had gone on during the week. However, as trust built in the group, they were able to use the group as a forum and a confidential place to share feelings rather than simply the facts about the week. Working with me in this first year and in the subsequent years were two other adults—the art teacher in the school program of the unit and a trainee in expressive arts therapy. Neither had experience in this kind of work, so each took their lead from me. I felt it was important for the staff to check in as well and to participate in all the activities with the teens. This kind of modelling was clearly invaluable to them. Sharing of staff needed to be personal, open, and friendly without taking away from the emphasis upon the teens' experience. It was a challenging position to maintain.

After check-in, we had a snack together, as the group was held in the mid-afternoon and carried on until suppertime. The snack period was an opportunity for further sharing and relaxed discussion. Sometimes teens brought taped music which they played during the snack time. Often issues would come up around whose tapes would be played that day. There was much heated emotion around different bands and types of music, and the teens found it difficult to agree. At times, taking turns seemed the only fair way to resolve the issue.

After snack, it was decided by the group that they needed a period of unwinding at this point. They found it difficult to sit and make art for the rest of the session. Considering this, we would spend about 20 minutes in the gym just burning off excess energy. It was interesting to observe the teens in the gym and what they would choose to do with their time. There were always those who threw themselves around with abandon—shooting hoops, playing floor hockey, etc. Then there were those who wanted one-to-one attention from staff; throwing a ball back and forth would suffice. Finally, there were those who felt intimidated by all of the vigorous activity going on and felt more comfortable sitting on the sidelines or drawing on a blackboard in the gym. Sometimes we would structure the time in the gym and develop an organized game in which everyone participated. Mostly, however, it was a free space.

Once we returned to the art room, we were able to focus on a structured activity which took us to the end of the session where we would check out. The check out consisted only of one word or sound or movement that expressed the sense of the group that day for each person. The predictable flow of the group activity seemed to help the teens. They took comfort in the structure and never questioned it. This first group played a major role in the development of the rituals, especially the idea of the gym time, so that they felt invested in the structures.

In setting the stage for the group, one of the major activities of this initial period was the development of group rules. With the consolidation of the group, a set of norms needed to be established. As one of the members took notes, the group brainstormed their ideas, mostly centering around safety. There was a discussion at this point about confidentiality. Naturally a group within the unit would have questions about how much they can freely share without feeling that we would tell the staff of the unit. Boundaries had to be established around information-sharing as well as around what is permissible in the group and what is permissible on the unit.

In the expressive arts therapy group, much more freedom was allowed than on the residential unit. Teens could swear in the group; this was quite important to them. It was my sense that in order for us to get more deeply into creative work, we could not be bound by too many restrictions. Like the rules that I have for individual work, there could be no hurting of others in the group. The teens were able to make the distinction between swearing as a way of letting off steam into the air and swearing that was hurtful to others by being directed at a particular person in order to make them feel inferior. There were humorous moments of much swearing at the end of the group all the way to the threshold of the doorway and then instantly ceasing upon passage through the door. This certainly demonstrated the capacity of the teens to recognize different expectations in different contexts.

Bounded yet free expression was a central working concept in the group. The bounded quality was reflected in the overall structure of the session, the flow from check-in to check-out and the rules and expectations. Because the teens participated in the creation of the structure and in the rule-making activity, it made more sense to them and they were more able to contain themselves from within. Free activity could take place without fear of things going totally out of control. Many of these teens were in residential treatment because of their lack of internal controls. Some carried diagnoses of conduct disorder, others of psychosis. Thus, the construction of a creative space that was clearly bounded but not rigid would be particularly important to them.

After spending the first several months of sessions on settling the group down, consolidating the membership, developing the structures, and generally getting to know each other, it seemed as though the group was ready to begin working artistically together. One of the first activities that we tried was the collective creation of a fantasy beast. Each teen made a part of a beast out of clay and hid it from view of the rest of the group. At an appointed time, we each put our parts together to create a whole beast. Of course, the beast ended up with several heads, but this was part of the experience. We next created a group story about the beast which was generated by taking turns, telling a part of the story in circular fashion until the group agreed that the story was finished. Fantasies flew in this session; and there was permission, within the frame, to be as wild as their imaginations allowed.

From this mutual storytelling and co-creation, we moved into what was to become the single focus of the group until the end of the year. Each teen made a mask. The process required that they do this initially with their eyes closed. The mask was first made out of clay, covered with plaster gauze and then painted. The process took quite a long time and encouraged a tactile relationship to develop with the mask. After the mask was finished, each teen constructed a story about the mask as if it were a character with an independent life. The following are examples of a few of the stories which were developed and the characters which emerged out of the stories:

The Unknown Child

I was born on a planet called NoName Planet. I had two parents that didn't look like me and no one on this planet looked like me. I was different. I had an older brother and his name was Mysterious and when I was three, my parents separated but my Dad still came around and caused trouble. And my Mom started going out with all these different guys. One of them said to me when I was alone in the room with him. He said that he wanted to do something with my Mom but my Mom wasn't around so he said that he wanted to do something with me. And then he left my Mom in the middle of the night so I don't know what happened to him. Then my Mom went out with this one guy and he got my Mom pregnant with my little brother and he got in a fight with my Mom and he left. Then one day I went over to my friend's house and I was playing outside in the backyard and her father said he wanted to see both of us for a second. So we went into the room and he wanted us to do something. He made us touch him somewhere not very nice. And I ran out of the house and my friend told me not to tell anyone because he would hurt us. A couple of years later when I was five, my older brother left home and then he went to some other place to live. When I used to go to grandmother's house, my uncle used to say: "Do you want to come into my room and see the fish?" So I went in. Sometimes my little brother came with me and he used to always put his arm around me. Then touch me somewhere where I don't want to be touched. One time when I was over at my grandma's house, my uncle David was making coffee and he put hot water

over my head and I went crying to my Mom and she
at first said it's only cold water. But then she noticed
he was making coffee. Then my Mom started yelling
at him. My grandma used to say that nothing happened
and she would stick up for my uncle. My grandpa
checked my head and said that it might blister. My life
now is OK. I told my best friend that my Mom was
hitting me and from there got right into CAS care. Right
now I live down on earth in a treatment centre. It's
the Alien Treatment Centre. It takes care of aliens. Now
I'm trying to deal with my issues. It's OK when I don't
have to talk about stuff but I force myself to get it over
with and get on with my life. I can talk when I know
it's safe and I won't get hurt. My name is the Unknown
Child.

This outpouring was totally unexpected. S. was generally
quiet and withdrawn in the group, although very present and
interested. S. had struggled for several years with depression
and suicidal feelings. She had attempted suicide several times—
once with an overdose of Tylenol and other times with slash-
ing and cutting of herself. She tried to swallow broken glass.
While the residential staff had been aware that S. had been
through the experiences which she related in thinly disguised
form in the story, S. had never been willing to share them with
other teens. She needed the shield of the mask to be able to
reveal herself. It provided the appropriate distance for her so
that she could both be and not-be the Unknown Child character. Her capacity to stay with this character and to eventually
play the role in collaboration with others was a significant step
for her.

Booster Gold Man

I was born on a pirate ship with lots and lots of pirate
people. One day when I was hanging around on the
deck (I was ten years old), something from outer space

came down and hit me on the head. It was a golden
leaf which changed my body into gold and then what
I did was I fell on the deck and I was looking at myself for two minutes and then I touched the railing and
it turned gold. Then the whole boat turned gold. After that I fell in the water and the water turned to gold.
Then all the pirates who were my buddies junped in
the water and then they started turning to gold and sinking to the bottom of the water. I couldn't stand on top
of the water so I sank down to the bottom. I died but
I'm a ghost and my ghost form is stuck inside the gold
body. I'm hoping that some day I can get out of it
and go to heaven or hell, whichever comes first. The
name people call me is Booster Gold Man.

For this boy, P., the group was initially quite difficult. He
had not really wanted to join the group at first, and the staff
had strongly urged, if not forced, him to be there. It was not
my style to force teens to join the group, so I was not invested
in whether he stayed or left. P. stood next to the wall watching the group for the first two or three sessions. He refused to
sit with us or to participate. He was willing to take his share of
snack and to run around in the gym. Slowly, he came closer
to the group, and his aloof stance developed into an interest
and curiosity about our activities. When he finally sat down
and joined us, it was beginning to be clear to him that he was
free to draw whatever he liked. When he realized that even
his drawings with messages written on them such as "I hate art!!!"
would be acceptable, he began to settle into the group and eventually took on a leadership role. His story, where the Midas-
touch of gold paradoxically ruins everything, especially prevent-
ing contact with others, reflects a damaged self, a ghost stuck
in a dangerous body. P.'s behaviour caused him great difficulty and was the reason he was contained in the unit. P. tried
to run away several times and often got into dangerous situations on the streets on his runaway adventures.

Sloppy Paint

Let's start off with the basics. My name first off is Sloppy Paint. A bunch of ooze was dropped on me when I was just a paint tray. Of course, humans had me with them all along and I ended up with a bunch of paint splattered on me and then I started to grow into a human shape. When I stepped outside for the first time, people asked me why I was such a mess and I replied: "I was made this way." Then everyone took off laughing. Then I saw this old man sitting on the street. He wanted to know where the nearest restaurant was and we were in the middle of nowhere. I turned to him and said: "I know about as much as you do." I was born in a paint studio. I'm turning fifteen in a couple of months. Before I was born, I was 400 years old as a paint tray. I was Michaelangelo's assistant. I held myself in mid-air so he could paint. I was glad when it was over. I don't like paint but I have to live with it because it's the way I was born.

D. had been living in the residential unit for almost two years when he began the group. D.'s family had basically abandoned him, and the unit was his only home at this point. D.'s art work often had an empty and disorganized quality. He had great difficulty connecting with other teens and often experienced himself as an outsider. His problems clustered around sexually inappropriate behaviour; and staff felt that they often had to watch D. to make sure that he did not act out sexually with other teens, both male and female. In our group, although D. was a bit isolated, D. seemed to have no difficulty in this respect and quite enjoyed himself.

After the construction of the mask and the development of their stories, we did some physicalizing of the characters. The teens explored the movements and gestures of the characters. How does this character walk? How does this character hold its body? How does it interract with other characters? We made a trip to the local thrift store and collected all kinds of clothing and accessories. The idea was also to dress as the character and then to explore movement in costume. We added text: does the character make a particular sound, does it say something over and over?

From here, we moved on to building this material into a drama which could be videotaped, both in its stages of construction and as a whole piece. It was difficult for the teens to stay on track with this, and it became necessary for staff to take more leadership in trying to shape the material into something coherent. We constructed the drama out of a series of improvisations which then were built into scenes and strung together into a form that loosely had a beginning, a middle, and an end.

The group process as we went along was interesting. The kids enjoyed the playful aspects of this co-creation. They liked to experiment with their costumes, helping each other dress and find just the right look. As we moved into some of the scenes, a leadership began to emerge based upon those members whose imagination began to flow most freely and who were willing to step forward and try to get the group to participate in their vision. People went along with each other and were intrigued by what could be developed. Those who developed as leaders were P. and another boy, J., who was quite meek and withdrawn on the unit. J.'s character was Rocketeer who has a jetpack on his back and flies out to rescue people in trouble. The image of this character was borrowed directly from a film that J. had seen. Although it was derivative and quite concrete, the character gave J. the freedom to "fly" with the other kids and actually to step out as a leader in the group.

The storyline was a fascinating one, considering the situation of all of these teens. Rocketeer and P. (before he is transformed into Gold Man) begin the story by crawling out of the sewers where they live. While walking around, they run into Sloppy Paint and Unknown Child who are wandering aimlessly. All of these characters are aliens and live on another planet. They meet and discuss the difficulties that are occuring down on earth. They've heard that earth is full of bad guys, and they feel that they are needed to go to earth and deal with the bad guys. So they get into a spaceship and take a very rocky ride down to earth. Along the way, P. falls out of the ship and is rescued by Rocketeer; during the rescue, P. turns into Gold Man.

When they arrive on the earth, the humans are in trouble. Bad guys (played by two staff members) are terrorizing the land. There is a scene in a bar where the bad guys are drunk and quite rowdy. Although they attempt to bully the aliens, they are rounded up by aliens and tricked into agreeing to go with them to the "Alien Treatment Centre." On the trip to the centre, the bad guys try to escape; and Gold Man uses his powerful golden touch to keep them in line. The aliens promise them that the Alien Treatment Centre will be a wonderful place, the place of their dreams; it will provide them with unlimited treats—candy, videos, etc. The bad guys are convinced, and the next scene takes place at the Alien Treatment Centre. Here the aliens now switch roles and play the doctors and nurses who are admitting the new residents. They are very stiff and formal, looking at their charts and discussing their patients' past behaviour in disapproving, clinical tones. Somehow, the bad guys/patients are convinced of the errors of their ways and, even though they realize that they will not be getting treats, they agree to stay and "work on their problems."

As we watched the video and discussed the drama with the teens, there was some sharing of feelings about the experience of entry into the residential unit. The teens agreed that they had felt tricked by their families and by staff into thinking that the unit would be a great place. They had never expected the reality of it; and, although it was not that bad, they still felt betrayed and abandoned to some extent. Mainly, they felt that they had no choice in the matter. These feelings were important for them to ventilate with each other, and the sharing of them brought them much closer as a group. I also felt that the opportunity in the drama to play out first their experience of alienation in general and second, what it might feel like to be staff and to see things from this perspective was a rare one. Shifting of roles is a central concept in drama therapy and one which worked very well in this case.

At the close of this first year of the expressive therapy group, there was much satisfaction both on the part of the unit itself and on the part of the teens involved. The teens were proud of their accomplishment in the drama and seeing it put together on the tape. They felt closer to each other and more engaged in the group. There was some sadness as one of the members, J., was leaving the unit soon. J. had been living there for almost three years; it was felt that before he became too institutionalized, he should move on. His mother was not willing to have him back at home, so he was going to a group home in the city. This last experience in the group was a positive one for J. and an opportunity for him to experiment with taking some leadership by stretching his imagination. Even to be able to express his sadness about leaving was a good experience for J. The staff on the unit were impressed by the way in which the teens had put their feelings into a dramatic form and, thus, were able to communicate to others. In presentations which we gave to the staff, they could see that the imaginal space had given the teens a sense of freedom and permission to tell their stories in a collaborative, creative way.

By the third year of its existence, the expressive arts therapy group had become a fixture on the unit. At every six-week review meeting where parents, teen, and staff come together to evaluate the teen's program, there was a report from the art teacher regarding the teen's progress in the group. Often staff would request art work to be shown, with the permission of the teen. Our work in the arts was coming to be appreciated and valued by other professionals who were beginning to be educated about this work and could see how important and useful it could be.

Each year's group had its own shape. The third-year group expressed the willingness to build toward a public performance at the end of the term. Although we had this as our goal, I felt that it was important to go through the process of slowly building the group in terms of trust and connection as a basis for any work that we attempted to do together later. In order to build the sense of the group, we reinstituted the ritual structure that we had from before—check-in, snack, gym, activity, check-out—and began talking about rules from the beginning. In fact, one of the new members (there were teens from the last year who were continuing as well as new members) said that he felt he might need the structure of a time-out for himself in order to contain his behaviour. We wanted to encourage this request and used it as a stepping off point to talk about rules as structures that help people to create more effectively. Some of our initial activities also helped to build group-ness: on a table-sized piece of paper, each teen had a circle drawn in front of them. The task was to put into the circle something that you would like others to know about you. The next step was to move from the inside of your circle with a drawing that connected to someone else's circle. Here there was an interplay between personal and collective space. To connect with others requires that I find a way to do it that experiments with ways to approach an other: intrusively, respectfully, gingerly, avoidantly, etc.

Another activity that we returned to was the imaginary beast. Each member made a part of the beast and we put all the parts together. A mutual story was generated in this group which was highly fantastical:

Once upon a time in a place far, far away there was a loud banging and trembling in the earth and suddenly it was—a new baby!! There was a monster with a strange sexuality. It doesn't know if it's a guy or a girl. The monster was walking down the road, heading for the treatment centre. On the way there, he took a pee on the road and a cop stopped him and asked him what he was doing. So he stuck his middle finger up. And then the monster with its one huge tongue wrapped his/her tongue around the policeman and whipped the policeman around and around in the air. After he swung around, he took the policewoman back to his place and then they were in bed. A week after, she was pregnant and she had a baby and they called it Fingers. One day Fingers met a girl and screwed her. And then they didn't stop until 1999 and so after realizing it was an extremely long time, Fingers decided to

go and seek help. He consulted a psychiatrist. The psychiatrist took a look at his cartoon brain and turned
some nuts and bolts and fixed him. He was totally
cured. But the problem was that the doctor had left
his wrench inside of Fingers' head and because of this
everytime that Fingers woke up unlike most teenagers
there was no sticky stuff. So he walked up to his Dad
and asked him for his sticky stuff. When Fingers asked
the Dad, his Dad said No. Fingers ran outside and
started touching all the women and saying "I want your
sticky stuff." A brick flew from heaven and hit him on
his noggin and he doesn't think about sticky stuff again.
Now all he thinks about is a clean peanut butter sand-
wich with olives. So he called up his best friend Michelle
Pfeiffer. Michelle decided to come over to Fingers'
house. Fingers got dressed up. He put on his best
ring and he went out for a night on the town with
Michelle. They had to decide what to do that evening.
In public. So Fingers said: "I would like to go and
have a sex change." S/he says goodbye to Michelle and
goes home to his/her father who sees that his son is a
daughter. She says: "Dad, will you marry me?" The
father says yes and they get married and have more children and the children grow up to be just like their
mother. At that time in the state of Illinois one could
not marry their parent, so the marriage was annulled
and the children were deleted. Both Fingers and his
parent were taken back to the original psychiatrist of
Fingers and the doctor did an autopsy and was completely devastated about the wrench in Fingers' head.
So the psychiatrist went to see a psychiatrist. It ends
up that nothing was wrong with the first psychiatrist so
he goes back to work. One night in his office out his
window he sees flashing lights in the sky. A burst of
light came from the flying saucer and went into his office. And there was Fingers. Then there was this guy
who came in and his name was Bruce [a group mem-
ber] and he was Fingers' father. And at that point Bruce
shot the psychiatrist. So then the Dad's wife came in

and said to Fingers: "Why did you want to marry your Dad?" Then he looked down. The wife said: "Look at you! Just look at you. Your zipper is unzipped."
Fingers said: "I hate to brag, but damn it's BIG!" So Fingers said that and the Mom (policelady) said: "What do you mean?" Fingers said "your gun" and shot everyone in the head, including himself.

The mood during the storytelling, as we kept going around the circle, was elevated and got quite silly. However, some real concerns were able to surface in the frame of the story; and, because we kept going *beyond the point of no return*, more and more concerns came up. There were issues of gender identity and confusion, resistance to authority, aggression and impulsivity, sexuality, incest, and certainly a great deal of violence. Even though these issues are so weighty and seriously concern these teens, the fact that they could be expressed with humor and as fantasy allowed them to come to the surface and be uttered safely in public. Humour can often serve to demystify some of this material and take away at least some of its power for awhile.

From this activity, we moved into the creation of individual fantasy creatures and individual stories about each creature. This work took a great deal of time and each teen was encouraged to stay with their creature until they felt completely finished. There was a sense that these creatures might eventually form the basis of the performance at the end of the term. The teens then developed stories out of the image of the clay creature.

The Thing From Outer Space

One day as a girl was walking to go to school, she came across something very unusual. So she went to investigate what it was. When she got there, she couldn't believe her eyes. It was something she had never seen before in her entire life. Standing in front of her was a huge totem pole-like monster. At first, she thought it was a statue. That is, until it ate her. Out of the blue, a loud noise shook the earth. The totem pole was moving. People screamed and cried as the large totem pole-like creature disrupted the poor town. People were squashed to death. Old people had heart attacks. Children peed their pants. But as the creature saw how much damage he'd done, it was shot. He fell over and crumbled. People cheered as they thought the creature was dead. But a little ways behind the body of the creature was an egg.

THE END

Stay tuned for the sequel!

Bloodclot

One day bloodclot woke up and got hungry. So he went to his friends house and asked him if he had anything to eat. And his friend said "No, but if you want to eat my cat, go ahead." So Bloodclot ate his friend's cat and he was still hungry. He's a major cannabalistic meateater and he's crazy about blood. After he ate whatever else he could find in his friend's house, he went to the opera theatre. The Phantom tried to stop him and he bit off the Phantom's head. So the Phantom tried to fight him without his head and then he ate the rest of him. That was the end of the Phantom. Then he went to his mom's house and his mother asked him what his problem was. And he said, "I'm hungry, man. I need blood!" And his mother said: "If you eat another living thing, I'll eat you." So he was still hungry, so he almost ate his mom. So she bit him right back and ate him.

Felix

There was a cat named Felix who sat on a rock and never moved. One day he saw a female cat go by. So he tried to get up off his rock but he could not do it. So he called the female cat over and said: "Call help! I need to get off here. I need a mutual life too you know." So she went and got help and he waited and waited. Four hours later, she came back with help. What kind of help you ask? Two cranes and a bull-dozer. So they pulled and tugged and pulled and tugged for days. But it was merely impossible. So they left him alone and the poor cat never had sex in his life for as long as he lived.

Screw Up

One day screw up was walking down the street and he got into a fight with another screw up. And when screw up got home, his mother called the police and screw up ran away from home. And he went to the home for the mentally screwed up. The first person he wanted to talk to was G. [the art teacher and group staff] because he thought that with all the jokes that G. tells maybe one of them could cheer him up and he could go back home. But the jokes were so bad, screw up had a heart attack and died.

Shithead

Shithead was a man and he worked in a science lab. He was working on an experiment to make people dis-appear and walk around as ghosts. So he was work-ing on his experiment and he tried it out on a mouse. The mouse dissolved like acid was eating him. Shithead was waiting there and he saw the wheel in the mouse cage turning so he waited for an hour. And the mouse disappeared. So Shithead decided to try it out himself. He took a little bit too much and he never reappeared again. So he went to a hotel and he went into this person's room and went under the bed. So he woke up the next morning and he went out for a walk. It was around 5PM and he was getting hungry so he went back to the hotel where he stayed and he went to the little fridge where he got food. And the person who owned the room walked in. She saw the fridge open so she went and closed it. Shithead was making all kinds of noises and the lady decided to go take a shower and Shithead went and got a knife and went into the bathroom and saw her taking her clothes off. She heard the door screech and she saw the knife. And she heard a voice saying: "Die, die." And she ran out of the bathroom past the knife. And the knife was chasing her down the hallway. She ran out into the lobby. There was a cop who arrested her for indecent exposure. So he got a cover and wrapped her up in it. He took her down to the police department and the chief of police went to the hotel and went up to her room. The cop opened the door and got stabbed with Shithead's knife. Shithead jumped out of the window and landed in the hotel pool. He drowned a lady and people were screaming. He went up to this guy and pounded him in the mouth and said: "Shut up, fuck face." Shithead reappeared and they called him into the police station for indecent exposure. They let him go after they charged him. And four years later, he died from somebody throwing shit in his face.

Stone Silly

One day Jesse James got stoned. He was walking by with Bob and he stopped and they started talking until he saw these legs pop up from a corner of a building. They saw this kid run out in front and then they heard this yell: "OOh, Mama! I wish you were my Mama!"

Then Cracked walked in and Cracked says: "You don't wish if she were your Mama because she's too old for you. She's 87. A Senior citizen. You wish if she were my Mama." And suddenly Cracked wakes up and he was having a bad dream and Cracked is dreaming that the old lady was going to be his Mom.

Cutie

CUTIE-PIE UNDER ARREST FOR VILLAINOUS MURDER OF YOUNG CHILDREN AND ADULTS!!! CAUTION: MAY APPEAR CUTE AND LOVEABLE BUT IS ONLY A DISGUISE AND UNDERNEATH LIES AN INCONGRU-ENT, SELF-CENTERED ANIMAL WHO CARRIES MANY GUNS AND WEAPONS. Such is the time of little Susie Jane. Susie Jane lived with her mother in New York and was a very good student. Often called "brainer" at school she felt lonely and unloved. Until Cutie came along and cheered her up. After a year, they trusted each other or, may I say, Susie trusted Cutie so much that Susie would trust her life to him and she did. She now lies in St. Clair Cemetery.

With the stories in place and a beginning sense of charac-ters emerging, we changed the location of the group from the art room to an open, carpeted space which allowed for more free movement. The group this year was beginning to coalesce. It seemed that many of the teens were interested in drama. Since there was no drama program in the school curriculum, we de-cided to focus in this area, as the teens seemed willing and ready to move in this direction. In addition, it was clear that the sto-ries had a great deal of action as part of their structure. For this reason, we realized that they might make ideal enactments. Our idea, as a staff, was to build on this raw material to con-struct a show performed for an audience.

The enactments were very successful. Each teen took charge of their story as if they were the director—inviting others to play various roles, shaping the action, adding new twists if they wished. Other teens and staff contributed ideas, but it was up to the "director" to incorporate or discard them. This gave the teens an opportunity to try out a leadership position. Of course, some were better able to handle it than others. Generally, there was much delight in seeing the story come to life and in using the frame of the stage to shape a drama. The transition from story to drama involved adding an element of conflict or sustained emotion as a focus. This transition also heightened the energy and commitment of the group members. The group made an effort to spend time and thought with each story and to make it as effective as possible. This activity had the ultimate effect of building trust amongst members. The trust was manifested in terms of the quality of the work.

We worked with the stories over quite a long period of time. When the date of the performance was scheduled, it came time to begin thinking seriously about putting something together. The teens decided that they were tired of the stories. We had spent the first part of our activity time in theater games and warm-ups, and this seemed to be what the teens enjoyed doing most. The staff came up with the idea of using these games and spontaneous warm-ups as the basis of the performance. This was where the life of the group was, and anything else might feel forced or stilted. The kids did extremely well with improvisatory work. They trusted each other enough and were free enough at this point to do some collective experimentation. The idea of using the warm-ups led to the notion of performing the group itself, actually showing the audience, which would be comprised of residential kids, other staff, and parents, what we have been doing over time in the group. Enacting the group involved a beginning (check-in), a middle (a series of activities) and an end (check-out).

In order to shape a stage space, we constructed a set which the teens decorated in grafitti style. The set provided an entry and an exit point; the doors and windows could be incorporated into the improvisations. Using the set in this way developed out of experimentation with props and incorporating objects into dramatic scenes. In one of the earlier groups we had used a table that served as a wall for an execution, as an elevator, and as a gravestone. The teens enjoyed stretching their imaginations in this way, and we thought that a set would also provide them with this opportunity. The set provided a sense of security and boundaries in terms of defining the space and also provided a stimulus to their creativity.

We planned that the check-in would be totally fresh on the day of the performance, and we encouraged the group to be honest even in front of an audience. In the activities section, we developed a structure. We began with some of the warm-ups we did in the group and then moved into spontaneously narrated stories that were acted out, scenes played in wildly changing emotions—called out from the sidelines—and open improvisations with themes (two guys in a sinking boat or a mother and daughter going for a frustrating clothes shopping trip, for example). We ended this section with a scene around a campfire and the telling of a mutual story, taking turns until each person had at least three turns. At this point in the performance, the teens were quite loose; and the material of the story reflected an ease and lack of self-consciousness around the audience. The check-out also was kept fresh and unrehearsed.

In terms of the feedback that we got from the show, the element which came across most clearly was the spirit of creativity and cooperation demonstrated by the teens. Audience members were swept up into the energy and spontaneity of the performances. Many of the observing teens expressed great interest in joining the group in the following September. All of the members of the group were interested in continuing, although many of the teens would either be moving on to another placement or attending school outside of the unit so that the timing of the group would not be quite right for them. It was obvious that the group process had lit the fire of creative excitement in the audience as well as the participants.

In reflecting upon the elements which made for a successful experience in this group, it seems that the time that was taken initially to build a sense of group-ness was crucial. Even though these kids lived together on an everyday basis, this particular formation and configuration of personalities needed to be shaped into a whole. Initial activities such as individual artmaking which then built into a group structure (the imaginary creature), the development of group rituals and a schedule which was repeated from week to week, and the creation of group rules and norms as both similar and different from the expectations on the unit, helped to forge a group identity. Once the group was formed and "normed," it was then possible to try to experiment creatively and take some risks artistically.

Drama seemed to be the modality which provided enough containment for free expression. Dramatic structures encouraged a great deal of physicality which was comfortable for most of the teens. They loved throwing themselves around with abandon. Since staff did not censor any of the material that the teens brought into the improvisations, their images tended to revolve around sexual, anal, and aggressive matters. The group would sometimes act as a self-regulator. Group members who often tended to sexualize scenes were booed by their peers, and the pressure of their disapproval would organically reshape the material.

In one case, F., a thirteen year old girl who was quite attractive and high-functioning, often found herself playing seductive women with quasi-southern accents. Her own love of the flamboyant, combined with certain boys who liked to sexualize scenes, sometimes created stuck or stereotyped dramas. F. was able to bring this to the group as an issue. She was fed up with always playing these roles, and she appealed to the boys to try not to encourage this in her. What was interesting was the discussion where both the girls and the boys could see how each was feeding into the other. The boys came to see that they were just as confined in their roles as F. The beauty of using the artistic form in a psychotherapeutic context is that such a discussion can take place on the level of metaphor. The dramatic form can hold a great deal of tension and conflict. The discussion we were having was about gender differences; yet formulating it in terms of roles in the drama, as metaphors for real-life choices, made it less personal and, thus, less threatening. Keeping the emphasis on the interaction between these characters and the impact on the audience was liberating for the group. They could actually feel, on a visceral level, that a stuck drama was boring and confining; and they could figure out how to get un-stuck by dropping the role and trying another one. The drama gave space to play and to experiment with different ways to be. For adolescents struggling with identity confusion, this use of artistic form was precisely what they wanted and needed.

Creativity: Mutual Recognition and Discovery

Several years ago a colleague of mine at the agency and I began planning to co-lead a group. We both felt that group therapy as a treatment modality had become increasingly underused since the rise and predominance of family therapy, especially in our agency. Just ten or fifteen years prior, there had been over twenty groups running at the agency. Until we began a group therapy program, there was only one group running as a holdover from the past. This group was an on-going women's group led by my colleague. She was assisted by a student co-leader who changed every year.

The new group that we envisioned was to be different from the existing women's group. My colleague, trained as a child psychiatrist, was also an artist. She was intrigued by the expressive arts therapy work that she had been exposed to and wanted to try working with me combining her depth of knowledge of group dynamics with my experience in using the arts in therapy. We were both struck by the number of children that we were seeing in assessments who had been sexually or physically abused or both. As we explored their histories, in interviews with the families, it also became clear that other family members had been exposed to abusive situations at some point in their lives. We felt that in some families the abuse had developed as a pattern of behaviour that was being handed down from one generation to the next.

To interrupt this "cycle of abuse," as we were terming it, we felt that intervention could take place on a number of levels. Family therapy was certainly important, and individual therapy for the child or parent was important as well. We also could see a role for group therapy for mothers of children referred to the agency, mothers who themselves had been abused as children. We felt that if we could intervene at this level, with the mothers in terms of their day-to-day interactions with their children, then perhaps we could begin to help families break the cycle.

It was our sense that group therapy might be especially effective in helping to break the isolation that many of these mothers were feeling in their lives. These women felt especially alone in regard to sharing material from their past. One of the powerful aspects of group therapy is the shared sense of commonality which can develop in the right kind of group. In a supportive atmosphere, people can be encouraged to talk about themselves. This discourse is powerful, especially in a group where others have had similar experiences. The feeling develops that one is not weird or strange but, rather, quite like others in terms of feeling and response. This can help people to begin to be easier on themselves and not so self-critical.

In the first year of the group, we read a great deal of literature on group therapy with women who have been sexually abused. It has been suggested that the way to work with such a group is to have a structured approach which follows a particular program. The establishment of safety for the women was, from this point of view, the most important consideration. Only after establishing safety could one then move on to cover a variety of themes, including anger, relationships, sexuality, and sadness. Taking this structured approach into account, we experimented with integrating art exercises into a highly structured format. I found this approach personally unsatisfying. The women came regularly at the beginning, so attendance was not an issue. However, the effect of so much pre-planning and deliberateness was quite deadening. We spent a great deal of time in discussion, and it was difficult to deepen the process so that real sharing began to happen. I felt that the structure was too rigid and did not allow for a flow from week to week. The topic would dictate the content; and while some of the topics were crucial (anger, for example), the action around the topic remained very "heady." Art activities were integrated but often seemed like illustrations of feelings rather than real expressions. By this I mean that the art activities were used like work tasks rather than having a life of their own. For example, if we were talking about anger, we would ask the women to draw a picture of the anger. This lead to predictable results. Thus, using art did not necessarily, in and of itself, yield deeper process. The group in the first year of existence was interesting but ultimately remained fairly superficial. I did not feel that we were tapping into the creative fire at all.

In the fall of 1993, we began another group which was an amalgamation of two different groups. One half of the group (subgroup A) were women who had come from the original sexual abuse group that had evolved over two years. By the second year of the group, members had changed and the group had begun to deepen. These women knew each other's stories and were comfortable with the art-making process which they had used quite effectively to explore issues in their lives. These women decided that they wanted to move on from the subject of sexual abuse exclusively at this point. They had already begun to move into other areas: in particular they were desperate for guidance and help with raising their children. All were single mothers living with scant resources, but all were devoted to parenting their children in a better way than they felt that they had been parented. The bonds that had formed between these women were strong and extended beyond the group itself. They sometimes saw each other outside of the group and their children knew each other.

The other half of the group (subgroup B) were women who had been in the on-going women's group. That group had gone through a transitional period where several members had decided to finish. The four women left were not yet ready to leave the group and yet they were too few to constitute a real group. When the combination of the two groups was suggested, all agreed to it. While this seemed like a straightforward solution to a technical problem, it created other problems which had to be addressed throughout the first few months of the group's life.

In the first meeting of the group, there were tensions between the two parts; and there was a certain amount of shyness and tentativeness as well. Subgroup A was delighted to be together again. They had a joyful reunion after the summer holidays. In subgroup B, one of the members, Diane, entered the room very angrily. We had some toy animals on the table. She took the biggest, fiercest dinosaur and used it to knock all the other animals down, saying that this was how she felt that night. Diane continued to refuse to participate that night. This had a profound effect on other people, especially Eileen who kept trying to reach out to Diane and help her. Eileen was in subgroup B and had a history with Diane. She tried to explain Diane's behaviour to subgroup A in order to help them to understand it and, perhaps, to help them relax around it. We introduced a sandtray exercise for this first meeting which generated some interesting material.

We asked each woman to take a toy and play with the others in the sand, creating some kind of a tableau together with the idea of the new group in mind. The following are some of the stories that were generated by the women:

Gina's Story (subgroup A)

Once upon a time there was a fierce dinosaur, long neck to stick in things and a long tail to sweep away what was behind her. As she thurped along she met a rooster who was crowing in broad daylight. She had stayed for a long time crowing until the prehistoric animal heard and happened along the path. Meanwhile a double-decker bus had lost its regular route but had decided to form its own route and happened into the same valley. Far away there was a small baby in the valley. She was lost and cold and afraid. The dinosaur, rooster, and bus knew that they had ended up there to find this baby. She kept saying that she was missing her twin. So the rooster stood on the bus as a look out. The baby went into the bus and the dinosaur followed behind, sweeping away their tracks, on the quest to find the lost child.

Eileen's Story (subgroup B)

I see a vegetarian dinosaur and his friend the rooster meeting again and happy to do so. The red bus is pulling away, ready to go off in a new direction. The rooster and the dino are closer than the bus. The baby is hiding—everything is new [too threatening]. If I hide, the dinosaur won't eat me, the rooster won't peck at me and the bus won't run me over. I feel abandoned just as I did as a baby. I feel abandoned by Diane, Tina, and Helen (members of subgroup B).

Felicia's Story (subgroup A)

I appear larger than life but in reality I am not a threat to any other being. I am sometimes aggressive and move right in. And though this may be scary for some, I do this based on my own fears. I am generally shy and gentle. I'm glad our group is changing and I know we will have ups and downs which at times will be hard. I want to grow.

Connie's Story (subgroup A)

This sandbox reminds me of the world, where old friends stick together and new friends feel that they don't belong. I know what it is to be afraid. I don't know what it is I could do or say to make Diane or Eileen feel more at ease. You do have a place in this group and you both are being accepted and welcomed by myself. And I hope that we can be new friends.

Setting up the sandtray and suggesting a way to move into it had a different feel to it than planning a topic and an activity for the group. The sandtray became the stage upon which feelings could be expressed as metaphors or in the form of imaginary enactments. Each woman had expressed her own vision and concerns about the new group and all had incorporated the strong feelings into her story. My vision of the sandtray as I looked at it, and which I shared with the group, was the following: *It is a dangerous place. A scary place. Stand firm, defend yourself. Face away. Show your teeth to the proud rooster. Baby hiding under the sand. Can't see. Protect yourself.* What I saw in the group's sand world was a stark picture of threat and defiance. There was not much softness or yielding in this world.

As the weeks went by, there was still a great deal of tension around the coming together of these two groups. Although she kept attending, Diane continued to keep herself apart from the group and to opt out of participation. This did not, however, stop the group from attempting to pull itself together. We created "rules" and worked with each woman's vision of what they wanted from the group We asked a four-part question of them: What do you want from the group? What stops you from achieving this? What do you need from the group in order to get beyond this place of stopping yourself? What kind of a group do you need?

Working on these questions helped to shape group interaction and sharing. Even Diane began to speak and share what she was feeling. What came up strongly when Diane addressed the question of what she wanted from the group was the sense that Diane hated art. She said she felt like throwing the materials and stomping on them. She saw herself as a cyclone which could damage others and therefore didn't speak at times for fear of hurting people. Diane felt she needed validation and needed not to feel afraid to speak. Diane had not realized that the new group would be using the arts so much; she felt angry about this. As time went on, Diane sometimes participated in the art making and other times would choose not to participate. I felt it was important not to force her to take part but to continue to help her explore the strong feelings that came up everytime we used the arts and to encourage her as much as possible to stay present in the group.

Eileen was quite clear in her answers to the four-part question. She expressed the desire to have some "backbone" in her life, to stop trying so hard to please others and to stand up for herself. What she saw as stopping her from achieving this was the fear of conflict and confrontation. She knew that she remained very private and secretive so that things would not go out of control. Eileen felt that she needed a supportive group to be able to work on these issues.

Tina's answers were somewhat similar to Eileen's. Tina felt that she was not good at standing up to people either, that sometimes she blew up at the wrong person, her son, for example, and this caused her much pain. Tina also feared losing control and feared being hurt herself. Without saying it explicitly, Tina also wished for a group that would be supportive enough for her to feel comfortable to work on the issues she was articulating.

Although there was still a sense of two factions in one group, as we moved into more content and encouraged participation, the group became much more interactive. After the first month, we planned to have a long group meeting. Our regular meetings were approximately one and one-half hours in length. Periodically, we found it important to add an intensive group of about four or five hours in length. This usually functioned to deepen the process and bring group members closer.

In the long group, we introduced a project which carried over into several subsequent weekly groups: we had each woman construct a box which represented the self that one presents to the outside world and the self that is experienced inside. Our sense was that the group was still in the forming stage and members needed some way to get to know each other better and on a less superficial level. The project acknowledged the fact that people have personae which they show to the world and also that they have private spaces inside which often re-main hidden.   We thought that for them to share both aspects of themselves would give them much more access to each other. The women took to the project immediately and worked stead-ily and intently on it for almost two hours. We had planned the project ahead of time, so some had brought objects and ma-terials from home for it. We also supplied all kinds of materi-als from paints to leaves and natural objects to fabrics to old magazines. Soft music played while they worked. Each woman was absorbed in her own world and the room was quiet. Even Diane was at work on the project, somehow not bothered this night that we were using art materials.

The results were striking. We sat in a circle and each woman took a turn passing her box around and sharing with the oth-ers in any way she wished. Gina chose a very small box to work with and filled it with tiny envelopes and containers. In-side these were pieces of paper on which she had written all sorts of contradictory statements, ideas, messages both good and bad. On the outside she had decorated the box with pictures of birds, glitter, stars and shiny things. The group responded to Gina's deep desire to be seen and recognized and her con-cern for the world as articulated clearly by the box.

Helen's small box was decorated on the outside like a Christ-mas present with a green pine branch. On the top she had placed an amethyst crystal on a soft green velvet cushion. Helen explained that the outside represented her need for life and growth as well as her desire for a more spiritual connection. Inside the box was a different story: Helen had spent much time on the inside, lining it with red tissue paper. Inside, nes-tled in the red paper, Helen had placed pictures from her child-hood. Helen had grown up in Latin America on a farm. The pictures depicted happy scenes of playful children and of Helen's mother walking through the farm fields with the children. For Helen, however, these scenes brought back very painful memo-ries. Inside Helen had also placed a small red bundle bound tightly. This bundle Helen called "my feelings." Next to the bundle was a picture of her son which she showed last. She expressed hopeful feelings about him, although there was pain as well around how angry she felt at him most of the time.

Gina gave feedback to Helen on her creation: she wished that Helen could bring the crystal inside in order to help her separate the past (painful family experiences) from the present (her current relationship with her son). She wished also that the "feeling bundle" could pop and let out its contents. Helen was quite moved by the experience of constructing the box and by the feedback she was given.

Eileen was the next to share. When she had heard about the forthcoming project the week before, Eileen had joked that probably her inside space would be blank. She was struck by how far from true this had turned out to be. In fact, her box was quite full on the inside and almost totally blank on the outside. Inside the box contained many pictures from her past, pretty things and a small writing book full of her calligraphy work. The pictures were of events and times that were happy and truly satisfying for Eileen. The atmosphere which Eileen created inside was rich, colorful and inviting. In contrast, she felt that her outside life was difficult and very painful. She was divorced from an abusive husband, living with her son and daughter who were demanding and problematic, and was without enough resources to live comfortably. At this point, Eileen was mourning the loss of her old life and her old self prior to her marriage.

Connie wanted to share but felt that she did not need much time. Her box, on the outside, also reflected a rushed quality looking stuck together and a bit fragile. Stuck on to the outside were magazine pictures of homeless people with messages written such as "the system has failed us" and "nowhere to go." Connie talked about her native origins and her deep connection to nature (the inside of the box) and how she wished that things could have been different in her life. Connie had spent much of her childhood either on reservation, living in a very difficult family, or in a training school for girls. She was a single mother living with her young son and working hard on not being abusive toward him.

Tina was the last to share that night. She had chosen quite a large box, the outside of which was covered with smiling pictures of her family and a copy of her best report card from grade school. Inside the box was a black sheet of paper with an explosion painted on it. Underneath this were pictures of her mother and of her son as well as sheets of paper with written messages on them. Large sheets had poems and stories she had written as well as negative messages, and there were a few tiny scraps with positive or hopeful words such as "self-worth", or "happiness" or "hope." Tina expressed the desire to make these tiny pieces bigger. She also spoke about the feeling of being locked up and imploding from the inside.

When we resumed the following week, Diane was the first to share. She had chosen to use a large glass jar instead of a paper box. The overall effect was quite human in its form. She had decorated the outside with yarn that looked like hair and then had spent much time making objects to put inside. These were stuffed pieces of fabric, some with pins stuck in them. She introduced her production as "Fred" and pushed it into the middle of the table with a dismissive gesture, saying it was "just a representation of myself, that's it..." When urged to say more about it, Diane said that the brain was frazzled, the lungs beaten up, the heart swollen and full of pins, the stomach full of pins and junk which created bad digestion. Shifting to speak more directly about herself, she said that she always felt sick with many aches and pains. Apart from the painful contents of her insides, she said that she felt empty, that her thoughts were in a whirlwind and that she did not feel her feelings. As "Fred," she spoke about having a sad smile but trying to look happy. Diane said that her father always had wanted her to be a boy and that her family was extremely unhappy. When she was young, her mother was diagnosed with a degenerative illness and things went downhill. There was no laughter, no playing, and the family eventually lost their house.

Diane received a great deal of support for her work. The group felt how important and significant it was that Diane was able to make anything and that she was willing to participate with everyone. The feedback that she was given was forthright and connected:

- glass could break, it's fragile.

- if you got rid of all the garbage, you could be or do anything.

- I don't feel close to you. You keep yourself separate from everyone. I'm trying to be open. I'm scared to be open, scared to be hurt.

- you really committed to making this.

- I like Fred's thoughts, swirling around, dark/light, masculine/feminine.

Felicia was the last person to share. The outside of Felicia's box was black and covered with white splotches of paint which she had made with her hands. She had put feathers on it which she said represented "honor and loyalty;" the black was "respect;" the white were the hands of others that tried to hurt her but could not get inside. The inside of the box was all white. Felicia felt that she was still "pure" despite all the things that had happened to her. In the space inside, Felicia had placed shiny ribbons to represent her children—three girls who lived with her and another child who was born when she was a teenager and whom she had placed for adoption. There were red splotches inside as well. These were the men in her life who had gotten inside and "tainted" her. There was a flower inside which, combined with the whiteness, reminded Felicia of her basic innocence. Felicia had been in many foster homes throughout her childhood and had ended up, like Connie, in a training school for girls. This experience in the training school had been quite devastating for her and, at this point in the group, she was beginning to be flooded with memories from this painful period of her life.

The creation of the boxes turned out to be a breakthrough experience for the group and made a big impression on each of them. Eileen and others said that they had thought about the boxes quite a bit in the intervening week. This simple action of making and sharing created a new atmosphere in the group. My colleague noted that the group seemed to be "melding" and coming together more. It was as if they gained a much deeper access to each other through the artistic process. It was my sense that revealing themselves in the language of the boxes—inside/outside—was a short-cut to material that might have taken much longer to emerge if we had stayed in the literal realm. Verbal discussion was important but only as an adjunct to the act of making and transforming experience through the manipulation of physical materials.

These women were clearly impressed with the creativity that they discovered within themselves and within the group. This discovery of their own power to produce something in the world that they could recognize as good was essential for them. They were, by and large, women who seldom felt as though they could have any impact anywhere. Living on welfare, trying to raise children without family supports or internal working models of successful parenting, left them without resources and often in despair. Art was a saving grace for most of them. The abundance of materials that we provided for them to make the boxes felt like food for the soul for them. Felicia, in particular, was seriously interested in art and she would often enjoy touching and stroking the paper that we provided.   She would sometimes take paper home with her and return with drawings to offer the group. Once she spent the money to have one of her drawings xeroxed so that she could give each member a copy.

As the group moved on from the experience of making the boxes, interaction between members began to increase. It was as if the coalescing of the group had allowed people to become more real for each other and to feel comfortable enough for issues between them to begin emerging. The art-making was certainly a catalyst for the deepening of group process. It also provided an opening where none existed before. It allowed members to become personal without feeling violated. The box provided a kind of cover or shelter—we could talk about the outside or inside of the box without literally talking about the person. Of course, the veil between person and artwork is a thin one. Yet they are really two different entities.

This perspective has echoes in the work of Shaun McNiff where he talks about the image as existing in its own right, independently of the self.

My sense is that the image and the self are *both* independent of each other *and* deeply connected. While it confines the image to think of it as only a projection of the self, it enhances its stature to think of it as having a life of its own. Once the box was created and put out into the world, it could divest itself of an entirely personal meaning. The box could be seen and appreciated by others for its aesthetic qualities. This is what gave each of these women their sense of pride and achievement. They felt that they had made something beautiful that could be recognized by others. They *also* certainly understood the personal meaning that the box had for them, and they could communicate this to others. In my view, image and self are only enhanced by their mutual co-existence.

In reflecting upon this group over time, it seems that there were several important elements that defined the group and helped it proceed. First, the importance of starting slowly and without a fixed agenda cannot be underestimated. There were exercises that we used to keep the process flowing such as the sand tray and the series of questions, but, by and large, we were not interested in pushing material in any particular direction. There were moments when new ideas were introduced by the leadership, but this was always in the interest of helping dormant and hidden issues rise to the surface more easily. We felt committed to helping the women in this group to take charge of their own lives; using the group as a laboratory for them to experiment with taking initiative was crucial. Thus, we resisted taking over from them.

Secondly, it was also crucial to be able to name the tensions that were arising because of the attempt to amalgamate two separate groups and make them into a whole. As leaders, we recognized that each faction had allegiance to its members and a history with them. Allowing the fears, fantasies, projections, and resistances to be expressed made things much easier and utimately paved the way for a coming together.

Thirdly, not pushing anyone into areas that they were un-willing to go was central to the spirit of the group. Diane had a strong negative reaction to art at times. I was tempted to cajole her or to persuade her or to analyze her difficulties away. I tried to catch myself and wonder about my investment in get-ting Diane to like art. If I was able to let Diane find her own way or experience the aloneness of sitting and just watching others, it was much better for both for her and for the group. Everyone then was able to get the message that they could be accepted and that there were minimal expectations coming from the leaders in terms of performance. Our stance then brought into relief their own individual expectations and the expecta-tions of the group.

Fourthly, I think that the interplay between heightened in-tensity and distance-making activity worked well in terms of cre-ating homeostasis in the group. Examples of a heightening of intensity would be the periodic use of long groups and allow-ing of conflict to emerge and flower. Examples of distance-mak-ing activity would be the use of reflection on individual and group dynamics and the reframing of conflict: it can be useful in that it teaches us about ourselves and about others. Art-mak-ing played a kind of in-between role in this respect. At times the artistic process heightened intensity and paved the way for a deepening of the interaction in the group. At other times, art-making helped to create distance and to de-personalize ex-perience.

This group continues to go on. Some of the members have left at this point and new people have joined. All of these women continue to struggle with their lives, but they have ex-pressed the sense that while the group is hard it provides them with an oasis space where they can express themselves in many different ways. Most of them came to enjoy using the arts and took great delight in discovering a creativity, a fire, long buried inside and untapped.

Creativity: Art-in-Relationship

From February 1985 to June 1986, I led an on-going art therapy group for women on Martha's Vineyard. There were seven participants, including myself as leader. We met one night per week during the first year and every other week thereafter. The core members were: Jane, a psychotherapist; Gabrielle, a painter and student in an art therapy training program; Martha, a psychologist; Sonia, a teacher; Susan, a clinical social worker; and Deborah, a musician and photographer.

The group had a certain structure to it, and we followed this structure or routine every week. I provided paints and simple art materials (markers, crayons, tempera paints, pastels, plasticene) and laid them out as people arrived. The two-hour session began with an hour of quiet time when they engaged in their own art-making. There was no conversation. My instructions were to paint or draw whatever came to mind, to number the pictures in sequence, and to note any associations to the pictures.

In this particular group there was not much interpersonal process. Interaction between group members was subordinated to the exploration of artwork by each individual. Other members would certainly give feedback to the person presenting their work, but the focus was always on the work in front of us and whatever was evoked by it. Often members of the group would be stimulated and affected by each other's work—a painting by one member would evoke a memory, a feeling, an echo of sameness or discordance in another member. Thus it seemed that no matter who was actually presenting her work, each one received something for herself from it.

I was interested in the impact of the context, of the group, on each woman's individual art expression. We often think of the creative artist as a solitary figure, struggling alone with a vision and trying to make it manifest in the world. We conceive of the artist as one who must reject relationship in order to create; otherwise there is the risk that the artistic process will be compromised. As the group proceeded, I could see that, rather than rejecting relationship to serve creative expression, it was in and through the texture of relationships within the group that creativity and artistic vision could emerge. Although there was not much interaction among group members, being present together and creating a holding space of mutual witnessing seemed to be where the creative fire burned. All of these women live on the island, and it was interesting to see how this context also influenced their experience of creative expression.

In order to get more information about the way in which the group provided inspiration for artistic activity, I decided to interview each woman and explore her story in the form of tape recorded dialogues with me. Each person speaks here in her own voice about the group and how making art in a context, in relationship, facilitated and enhanced creativity. These dialogues took place several months after the group ended. I have edited them to bring the issues into sharper focus.

Jane

The formation of the group coincided with a period of transition in Jane's life. She had been practicing as a psychotherapist for some time on the island and then had a child. Pulling inward and toward her family for several years was beginning to give way to moving out into the world. Her child was older, and Jane was beginning to stretch her wings, travelling off the island to attend conferences, trainings, workshops, cultural events. This movement away was creating tension in the family, and Jane was in struggle with the imbalances that were emerging for her and her family. Jane was in an intense period of experimentation with new ideas and was taking many emotional risks. Her use of the artwork involved sorting out some of these life changes and exploring all the possibilites.

EL: What role does the art-making play in some of the changes that you are going through now?

J: The art was a way for me to experiment with another form of expression. I liked that it has a nonverbal element. Movement had become increasingly a part of my life. Meditation was the same process, incorporating the religious mode. It was a coalescing of many forms and spaces of holding a broader, deeper expanse. Also, conventionality and unconventionality are the two contradictory poles of my life right now. Over the past three years, there has been more activation of this dichotomy. I am expanding in order to integrate them and I have no idea where I will be in three or four years. I am going to the edge to really experience the largeness of this expansion. I was using the art to explore some of this.

EL: What impact has this had on your family, your marriage?

J: At first it was threatening because it was unknown. It left a lot of questions because it shakes up old ways of doing things. But it is also a modelling for my child. It shows that there are possibilities for energy to go in new ways. It is clear that each person has to undergo their own transformation. In a relationship a lot of aliveness is available if each person does it. But each person's risk level is different. My husband has accepted the invitation to enter his own process, and he is knowing me better. Whatever our common path, there are possibilities, but the actual shape of our relationship is in transformation now. I personally am compelled to go forward even if this means leaving behind everything I know, all the structures.

EL: Let's look at some of your artwork to see how you used the experience. What about the process of the group? Did it enable you to do some of these pictures more easily?

J: The same thing happens in the art therapy group that happens in love, the therapeutic process, in sharing a work of great music. It is a nourishment, a being known and knowing, a mutual sharing that we are larger than our forms, than our substance, that we are all out of the same nature. Like these other experiences, being in the group is for me the sense of coming home.

EL: So the group provided a safe place for you to take some risks, and it was a vehicle through which you could be in more touch with deeper parts of yourself.

J: Yes. For example, in this one (Figure 1), my life is in total flux and I am saying "yes" to it. I am making the commitment not to take the safe, old paths anymore and to be willing to be on the edge and to develop the trust, the will, to surrender. I want to have humility, aliveness, serenity without knowing.

Figure 1. (Jane)

EL: It looks like you are getting more comfortable with the paint here and that could mirror your inner experience as well.

J: Sometimes in doing the art, I found an aliveness without judgment. I love the feeling of this. Letting go. When I get into a deep meditative state, my breath comes out of the top of my head. Oneness, the sea of passion.

EL: It seems that your paintings help you to get a little more specific about the internal process that is unfolding, but they are as open-ended as the process itself.

J: Yes. In other ones, there is continual opening and continual vulnerability. The elements of life change the course of time. There is fire and ice—the flames surround but do not consume. The contradictions exist together in harmony, and there is a certain softness.

Gabrielle

The group was an important support system for Gabrielle, both for the creation of her artwork and for the major life moves that she was making at the time. Gabrielle had wanted to study art therapy for many years but had never been able to do it for various internal and external reasons. The formation of the group coincided with her decision to return to school as a mature student. Studying art therapy meant that she would have to leave the island every week and stay away for several nights. It also meant negotiating the city on her own, separating from the island and all that was "safe." Issues of dependency and independence many adults typically deal with in adolescence were emerging for Gabrielle at a later age. Going off the island was a big event; she had never driven off the island alone before. Every week, Gabrielle would use the group to give her more encouragement and to listen to her tales of interviewing, of being accepted, and then of undertaking the program. She found strength in the group generally and, more specifically, through the artistic process as it was carried forward by the group. As an artist, however, she found that the art-work she produced in the group was quite different from the work that she produced alone in the studio.

EL: Did you feel that you were creative in the group?

G: Oh, definitely. I found seeds in this that I probably would not have found alone at home. I allowed myself to accept the group situation and this made my artwork freer, more allowing itself. The experience of having others sitting around and knowing that they are all doing it together is so important. Also the allowing of time for sharing with each other—beginning with an openness to whatever will happen and just letting it happen. I'm even doing that more and more with my work teaching art to children. I give up my plan for that day and just sit with them and let them tell me what they want to do. More interesting and creative things happen that way. When the group ended, that was the end of this kind of painting. In my own painting, I have been trying to allow in the way that we did in the group. An "allowingness thing." Going outside of your own patterns.

EL: How do the paintings that you do in your studio now reflect what you are calling this "allowingness thing?"

G: The paintings that I do now and the ones from the group bring me back to a period in my life when I lived in Mexico and did some painting and sculpting at a school there for about six months. It was a very free time in my life. All my friends there were artists. I can't explain to you very clearly what my paintings now are about but I can give you a sense of the images. In many of my paintings there is a great deal of movement. For example, in this one (Figure 2) there is a pushing movement, black waves, prickling spines. Circling, swirl-force, pressure-eye, outthrust, red blood. Another one that I did expresses the feelings I had about a friend who was dying of cancer. She happened to be visiting the group one night: breaking, black lines but allowing the white space to stay, shapes are for their own sake, a lot of conflict. Jagged. Pools of tears, sadness, anger. Disturbance of feeling about the way that cancer was running all through her body. I painted a lot of eyes: the all-hearing, all-seeing eye. The shape is intriguing to me. I use it a lot. I don't know why. The eye feels very forgiving.

Figure 2. (Gabrielle)

EL: What is forgiving?

G: Accepting who I am. An open eye. An eye of allowing, of being. This one (Figure 3) looks like a human form, giving birth. There is a lot of birthing going on in all of these.

Figure 3. (Gabrielle)

EL: In terms of process, did you come to the group with a sense of what you needed to paint?

G: No. Every night was different. I just let whatever happened happen. It was always a surprise. Haptic outpourings. No plan.

Martha

It was mainly a desire for further knowledge and under-standing of the field of art therapy that initially motivated Martha to become part of the group. She had studied some art therapy as part of her training in psychology but, since coming to the island thirteen years before, she had not had much opportunity to pursue work in this area. The group sessions took place at her home and she made sure that the atmosphere was welcom-ing, helping to set up and providing tea and freshly baked cook-ies every week. Martha certainly contributed to the comfort-able ambiance of the group.

For the first year or so, Martha was quiet and private, de-clining to share her work for the most part. Her keen interest and total involvement in the process was evident, but she chose to remain separate and outside. It was always my sense as the leader that I would not push anyone who did not feel ready to share her work. I gave each person the opportunity to share by inviting them gently; but, if they declined, I did not go any further. I think that this attitude toward the process made it possible for some of the women to stay with the group and to trust more easily. Martha felt pushed in other group therapy experiences, and she was wary of this group in that respect.

EL: How was this group different from the other groups that you had been involved in before?

M: I have always been very comfortable with my hands. I like to be doing something. Everything frees up for me if my hands are busy. I feel safer. So I knew that I would have a good time with art materials in this group. In other groups there was no space for me to be who I was. There was great pressure to conform or what I felt to be conformity, under the guise of asking us to be free. I felt very cramped by that and I became secretive and almost rebellious in that kind of passive/aggressive way that children can be. But this group was different.

EL: It is interesting that the group was such a safe medium for you.

M: Very safe. Because as long as I don't talk, it's safe. I know what's there, but who else knows?

EL: So the danger comes with other people knowing and other people seeing.

M: That's right.

EL: And then what could happen?

M: ....being contaminated by it.

EL: And then you couldn't control what they would think.

M: What they would think or what might happen to them. It's more what would happen to them, that something on the paper would contaminate them. And in the case of one or two of the paintings in the group, from time to time I have felt very threatened by other people's images. Some material came out that was very destructive and very threatening to me, and very chaotic. And I couldn't look at those paintings. I would often look away, or I would look quickly, or I would look at them from the floor so that the painting would be different. I didn't want to be drawn into those frightening turmoils.

The group had to be a safe place for Martha. It was crucial that the group be safe enough for her to enter her unconscious through art and to discover what was there. She regarded the experience as an opportunity to play in the context of the group rather than with the group. Vulnerability and exposure are important themes in her art-work. For a long time, sea creatures, especially mermaids—half-human and half-animal—were present in her art-work.

M: The mermaid (Figure 4) is a part of me, so much me. It separates me from the others...This mermaid is in a fetal position, in a womb where she is safe and protected. I have to be careful how I behave, I feel too visible...I have had to learn some secretiveness through my life experience but my instinct is to just put it right out there. I am always afraid that I will let things out that I shouldn't for some reason. This is disconnected even from the job. I feel that I am just too much like a jellyfish without a skin and people can see right through me. That's how I am; but I feel that propriety expects you to pull a windowshade down on that kind of visibility, that it's somehow not what we're supposed to do in the world.

Figure 4. (Martha)

EL: What did the group help to free you up to do? Were you working on any particular issues in the group through the work?

M: I was looking at my job and thinking "where do I go next?" Because I have been doing the work of one and one-half people, I've become aware that the job is just very taxing physically and that I have no way of leaving it. Living on an island, I can't get away to the next town. I was thinking about whether I should stop. Yet playing with it on paper, I could see so many things about it that were valuable to me. Too valuable to leave yet until I found the next thing. So that process helped me. I sort of found that I wasn't ready to leave it.

EL: What else are you expressing in your artwork?

M: I think I was also exploring my own sense of vulnerability and the feeling of being different or strange. A feeling of danger in the world. This comes out in naked figures or in pictures of children.

Martha had been taking part in workshops on kindergarten screening procedures where she felt that there had been too much emphasis on putting children in rigid age categories. She did a picture that represents the notion that children who should be flowering are being forced into alien boxes. The flower is the children as they should be, thorny as well as sweet. Children should grow like flowers and not be constrained onto a trellis. In many ways, this is a metaphor for Martha's experience of the group.

Sonia

Like Martha, Sonia needed a quiet, safe space in order to create with art materials. Sonia worked as an elementary school teacher and experienced her job as very stressful and hectic. She was also going through a divorce, although no one in the group knew about it. She needed to feel that the group was not putting pressure on her in any way, and she declined to share her work in the group. Like Martha, Sonia was fully engaged in the group process despite her lack of overt participation. Her paintings reveal a great deal of inner process and a strong connection with the group. In reflecting about the group, Sonia and I discussed her position as a participant-observer.

EL: I felt your engagement. Is that true of your family also, that you were watching yet very connected?

S: This is new learning for me. Now knowing what I know about the children of alcoholics, I always felt that being the youngest child, I saw all the mistakes of my other siblings; and I wasn't going to do the same thing, get pulled in.

EL: Was it the conflict, not wanting to get pulled into the conflict?

S: Or also the competition. They did everything, and they were all successful. I didn't want to risk so I held myself back.

EL: Is that what it was like in the group?

S: No, not really. I think that the reason I didn't participate verbally was that I initially came into the group just to see what you did. I thought that I was coming to be taught techniques. Once I got there and saw what you were doing, I knew that I could learn from that. Then you can't help but get into it. But as time went on, I felt that it was alright not to speak.

EL: It was alright with me too. I spent some time thinking about this, about how I should handle it. At first, I was concerned for you and I wondered whether everything was OK with you I knew it would be difficult for you to talk after remaining silent for so long. I thought about talking to you privately about it and decided to give it time. Then, at a certain point, I realized that you were fully present. I could tell by your body, the fact that you never missed a group, and your engagement in the painting.

S: Yes. And that amazed me. I had never done that kind of painting before. I can't remember grammar school. My painting had always been formal. I can't remember anything personal. But I did hate to come. It was such an effort because my days were so exhausting, a big workload. But once I got there it was a very special inside time.

It was like having a vitamin pill. Not just relaxed and refreshed but also an emptying out. A nice thing to do.

EL: Did your paintings resolve issues for you?

S: No. I would always take up the same themes again and again and work on them. For example, on this one (Figure 5), which was the first one that I did in the group, I wrote: "My tree. Reaching out. Warm. To you all sitting over there."

Figure 5. (Sonia)

EL: I almost felt that you came in and set up this space around yourself and that space was clearly yours. But other people were welcome. I didn't feel that it was exclusion. There was a sense of a bubble going down around you. And here in this picture it is very warm. There is a sense of wanting contact.

S: I did want it. I remember that. I remember this night very well because I didn't know what you were about, and I didn't know what was expected or what you were doing. I just decided to do my thing.

EL: So the group seems to be having an impact on your work.

S: Yes, and there is a strong connection for me between my feelings about art education, spirituality and life. Also nature is crucial for me. I grew up in the woods, and the woods are really in my soul.

EL: So it is interesting that the first picture that you did in the group was a tree.

S: Most of my paintings are trees! I once took a course taught by Uri Shulevitz on writing and illustrating childrens' books, and I wrote a book called *A Tree*. It is about a child sitting in a tree observing life. Isn't that amazing, the idea of seeing your neighborhood from your tree?

EL: In this picture, you are the tree and the arms of the tree are reaching out. Is there a sun behind it?

S: I don't know why I did that—maybe just to get it to look warm.

EL: I wonder what effect the environment had upon you, being in someone's home and the warmth created by that.

S: I'm sure that it was significant. In some paintings, I addressed particular issues in my life. In one important one, I explored my reaction to the divorce; and it was done on the night I went to court to get my divorce but no one knew about that. I painted my door, the one through which I was going. And I didn't know what was going to happen next. It's all white out there; I wanted it to be white. This was the same night as the previous painting. I think the one thing I did say in the group was that I kept trying to paint things bad because I knew it wasn't all going to be wonderful in my life with the divorce. But it was wonderful, and that's what made it hard for me to talk in the group. Other people had things that they were trying to endure. I didn't. There was nothing that I was enduring then. The hardest part for me had to do with the kids. I knew it wasn't going to be smooth for them.

I've always had the feeling that life is a dance. So a lot of my paintings are dancing in various ways. I did one where the associations were: "Sculpture, helper me, help up, someone who is getting up, inside me, resting open and shut, me with others, action, me holding, covering, protecting me." I paint this a lot. This is me. Can you see my arms? This is my body.

EL: It's all of you. Someone who is getting up. I think that is very interesting. It feels like that's what is happening in your life. You are getting up, starting to rise up.

S: But I have community deeply within me—how we all fit into it and how we all are it. This is very important to me.

EL: So in this painting there is a lot of interaction going on. You are holding it together. I sense that during this period of splitting up the family, there would be a need to hold things together.

S: Yes. I was very busy trying to get it all to hold together on the paper.

EL: The surfaces and the background. Trying to keep it from flying apart. You've decided to end the marriage and have taken this big step and then praying that it somehow stays together, especially for the kids.

S: You're right! I sometimes did what I call flat pictures. This is the way I usually entered the group and started off.

Susan

Susan was a relative newcomer to the group and had not been on the island very long. She joined us in the middle of our second year and was interested in the process of art as therapy, both as a therapist herself and as someone who had done art-work on and off for some time. Susan had always been attracted to art as a way of connecting to her inner life, and she was also searching for community and relationships on the island. Thus, for her, the group served several purposes.

The particular issues she was facing in her life at the time of the group involved learning to live independently, supporting herself in a full-time job, as well as dealing with depression— finding the sources of her energy and her anger and being more expressive.

EL: How has the group had an impact on you?

S: It has done a lot for me personally. My arm tapping into what is inside my head and then putting it out on the paper. I have done some of this with my clients, especially the kids that I see. One woman I see brings in things that she paints outside of the session and we discuss it. I have drawn along with some patients. One woman is an incest survivor, and she drew a picture of herself and her father together when she was a little girl. She didn't realize that she didn't put any neck on herself and that the head was separate from the body. We talked about that. It really clicked with her that her thoughts and her feelings are separated, that there is no connection between those two levels for her.

EL: It may stem from early experiences where she had to disconnect the feelings from her body, otherwise she could not bear it.

S: I'm working mostly with women now and with a lot of women who have been sexually abused or incest survivors.

EL: Were you ever abused as a child?

S: I know I was physically abused, emotionally abused for sure. There were some boundaries that were not respected by my mother. Borderline situations that did not give me ownership over my own body.

EL: Space to be separate and not an extension of her.

S: Yes. She always said that I was so much like her. So my whole process in the last 20 years is to try to be me, and I am still working on that. It's very hard, painful.

EL: Any sources of joy in this?

S: Not much. From working on myself, from breaking through things, sometimes I feel good.

Susan's paintings are reflections of some of these issues. In the first group that she attended, she brought in some pictures that she had done at home. The first drawing (Figure 6) depicted a scene from a dream.

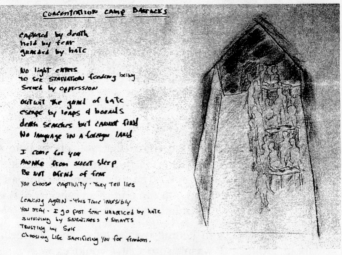

Figure 6. (Susan)

S: This is a dream about a concentration camp. I am trying to get out and to get a friend of mine out. A lot of people around me are resigned to being there and they have no ambition to escape. There is a male figure at the back and one at the front. The guards are dumb even though they have weapons. It would be easy to get out. Other people were passive, like blobs, no desire left. Do I have to be like them? Why don't I take the risk and get out? It's so symbolic. I have gone along with the crowd. Not following my own desires or my own questioning, being who I am. I would rather be the one who is free. The crowd keeps me back, wanting to be like everyone else, and accepting that.

EL: This seems like an inner conflict that the dream represents: your own passivity and the depression that you spoke about earlier—that's the crowd. Your intellectual powers give you the capacity to see where you could be but the other forces are pretty powerful and hold you back. The depression is dumb; it is numb also. Something is telling you that it is easy, so easy to get out.

S: I felt like a nothing or nobody and unique at the same time as a child. The specialness helped me to survive in a way. Being apart and a part of the crowd. I have great difficulty in groups. Five or ten years ago I could not stand to be in groups, but this has changed.

EL: Are you in this picture?

S: No.

EL: Looking above. And the colors that you chose here express a lot. Escaping from the position of being in it and out of it at the same time. The art therapy group had already formed itself and you came in as an outsider—so you must have had some feelings about this.

S: I've done well with getting over a lot of the old feelings about groups. I wasn't sure that I could express what I wanted to express in the group. But I was not apprehensive about it. Another one that I brought with me when I came into the group is a picture of a woman standing above the clouds and dispersing stars. It reminds me that I have a lot to give if only it could be tapped. Symbols in the picture—infinity—never-ending universe; femaleness, throwing out stars, numerology—33 stars: a pure number, the most pure and spiritual number. The higher self. After I drew it, I realized that it looked like my body only 20 pounds thinner. I wanted to continue with an image from an airplane with the clouds evenly dispersed. It reminds me of an article about a Russian cosmonaut seeing angels in the sky with large wings.

I did another parts picture, experimenting again with drawing things. I didn't know what to do that night and started
with a hand and an arm. I don't know who it is. I don't
like it very much. It's too disorganized, disheveled, frenetic.

EL: If this person could speak, what do you think he or she
would say?

S: Something about pain and sadness. The face loks pained.
The gesture of the arms looks exposed. It's a male person.
I did one that just depicted faces. I like this one pretty much.
Except for the black ones. They look too gruesome, disorganized, psychotic. They are disintegrating. Eventually, I
get it together, though. The ending is not scary, more like
a video image, more creative use of line and more organized.

EL: Here you are using the art to reassure yourself that you are
OK. I get the feeling with your work that you do a lot of
inner exploration.

S: Right. It's like creating myself. Reintegration. In one where
I painted for the first time in the group, I made something
that looks a little like cave paintings. A bull. Taurus,
strength. Opposite of Scorpio, which is what I am. My
father was a Taurus. I've never known that many.

EL: You need a lot of strength to deal with your life on the
island these days—being on your own, handling a stressful
job. You are drawing on the images in your paintings to
give you power.

S: This last one (Figure 7) is another woman in the sky but
her gifts are coming from a different place! This is a yoga
stance. The energy is coming from the heavens and passing out of me. I am giving birth to shell, whale tail, butter-
fly. Symbols are like hieroglyphics, things of the earth.

EL: This is powerful. Do you think of yourself this way in fantasy at least as being the intermediary of life-energy?

S: I don't think of myself this way but I think of all human
beings that way.

Figure 7. (Susan)

EL: It is interesting to compare this one to the other woman in
the sky that we have already described. The colors are similar, but the first one is much more from the head, thinking,
above it all. This one is more of the earth. Put the two
together, first one on top of the other. Here we have quite
an idealized image.

Deborah

The group had been in formation for almost a year before
Deborah joined us. She seemed to feel at home almost immediately and was very gregarious and outspoken. However,
Deborah did not initially feel comfortable with her paintings.
She judged herself in relation to the others on many levels: she
"wasn't an artist;" she "hadn't been doing this so long;" she
"wasn't a professional;" she "wasn't a shrink like most of you,"

and so forth. As the group gave her support and extended it-self uncritically toward her, she became less self-conscious and more aware of how she put herself down and tended to de-flect her energy. She was able, at times, to joke about her shaky feelings or her feelings of competitiveness in relation to the oth-ers, and this gave her the distance and control that she needed to function actively in the group. Deborah was born on the island and was the only native islander in the group, still living on her ancestral lands. At the time of her entrance into the group, she was beginning to recover from a painful divorce that left her a single mother to two young children. Coincident with the divorce, she had spent some time in a psychiatric hospital suffering from severe depression. Deborah had been involved in some art therapy while she was in the hospital, and it had affected her deeply. Like Susan, Deborah brought some paint-ings into the group with her. Perhaps they were like offerings and ways that she could locate herself with us.

D: I did a group there called "Experimenting with Art" and I was the only one in the group for some reason. I had a chance to really make a connection with the leader, and she was the first person who could reach me in the hospi-tal. She had me draw my feelings....a big black spot and crumpling it up and stomping on it and screaming. It was a great two hours. I realized that art was my ticket. And even though that art group was only scheduled twice a week, I asked for a daily session. It really worked for me. It was the way I climbed out of the deepest, darkest black hole in the world. I did a picture when I was in the hos-pital for the first time during the second week, when I was really in excruciating pain. I call it the 'Crying Tree.' The leaves were falling from the trees. The pine needles were falling. It looked like tears and the tears were welling up from the deepest part of the earth. And I was identifying with my own original pain in the womb—of having my Daddy leave me, which isn't technically how it happened but how I experienced it. What my therapist said to me was: 'You may be depressed but take a look at this. It has bal-ance, and color, and life!' What I'm aware of is that it is a beautiful tree. It has grace and integrity and even though it's in excruciating pain, it's not dead. It's very much alive, and ....it goes back to the earth and replenishes the root system. This stream that I see here...this stream is the stream of life that we're all connected to, that all of our roots tap into. It's the common pain that we all feel. It's the same pain, it doesn't matter what the circumstances or the details are.

I did another one maybe a month later, a week before I had my psychotic break. It was December then. It was what the winter sky looks like to me, especially in the city— at rush hour—seeing the trees and sunset. Three trees, bare of leaves standing against the sunset sky. What came to me a few days later was that it was the new shape of my family, three of us rather than four of us. It was one of the ways I needed to see that and understand it. I was struggling with it and having a very hard time with it, being a family of three. So this is an affirmation.

This was the first one that I did in the group (Figure 8). I love this and keep it on the wall of my bedroom. What a difference from the other trees!

EL: There it is, standing there, very massive, right in the center.

D: Bold, strong, surrounded by and part of life and light. A solid base.

EL: Is that the sun coming up behind it?

D: That's the sun. And it's attractive. I like it.

EL: Do you remember your experience on the first night, what you were feeling?

D: Oh, I loved it. I loved being there. I knew it was the right place to be. I knew I would really thrive there. I remember I shared my stuff right away. It felt like I was taking a risk because I didn't know anybody. But I felt welcomed right away. It felt really good. I also know enough about this stuff to know that if you don't enter into it, you don't get as much out of it.

Figure 8. (Deborah)

EL: That's right. In a way, this first picture is your statement about yourself to the group. Presenting, Deborah! It's a strong statement.

D: I did this picture at a time when I needed to remind myself that I was...am strong, independent, self-sufficient. No matter what I've been through, this sucker has not been felled yet.

EL: We don't have any trees that have been chopped down in your pictures.

D: I don't even see a scratch on the trunk! I was able to see that some of the problems in my life were merely rustling in the branches. The branches would wave and some leaves would get blown off and there would be a storm here and there, but the root, the core, was never disturbed. Also, what came to me much later is the idea that there is so much up here that you can't see yet. There is more.

EL: Yes. The tree is going off the page into some potential space that we don't know about.

D: There is more to come. It's not finished. There is another one that I did with a similar theme. It is a painting of the horizon with black on the bottom and sunrise on the top half of the page. What I ended up feeling about it was endless possibilities. The balance of light and dark. A solid base—dark and light exist in relation to each other. Also this looks like a desert or twilight. Having everything laid out before you, endless possibilities. I think that Jane said it looked like the sea in the early morning when it is black. The horizon, the edge is the endless possibility.

EL: I guess you don't want to go to the edge unless you are feeling like you are not going to fall off.

D: Right. And, speaking of protection, this one (Figure 9) is called "The World According to Deborah!" This started as my bubble.

EL: Did you start with the round shape?

D: Yes. It was a bubble because Martha used to talk about being in her own bubble. That was a nice image so I started with that. It was a time which I needed to reaffirm that I was safe. Again. A little like the house with the trees around it. I was also feeling good about my room. I was in the process of hanging pictures, making mobiles, finding a quilt at the dump and repairing it. Feeling like I was making my nest. I like the roundness of it, wholeness, completion, self-contained.

EL: It seems very harmonious and balanced. It's your time to be in the middle. It's your time of life to be more in the center. You are making yourself more of a priority here.

Figure 9. (Deborah)

D: In terms of the painting, I think I've included everything that is important to me with my music being the focus in my life—my family, light, plants, my telephone, my journal, my books, my association with the church. This picture is a real fulfillment of being happy alone. But...the support of my friends is still important. I can't do it without the support. And another issue here is that I want to share all of this with somebody some day. My parents separated when I was born and my father died when I was eight years old. I never knew him and just began several years ago to think about him. He was a professional musician and a violin maker. I inherited some of his gifts—working with my hands and music. I intend to use music and art to touch other people. An important picture that sticks in my mind is one that I did of my dulcimer.

Deborah brought her dulcimer to the group one night and sang for us. She spends her time playing music and singing with the elderly as well as with young children. Deborah talks of possible further study in the area of music therapy.

Many of the women in this group were in a transitional period in their lives. What was central for them all was the experience of a quiet, sheltering space in which they could go inside themselves through the art. These women created in the presence of each other. This mutuality generated a feeling of acceptance and allowed them to feel free. The creative process for the women in this group placed a value on respect, support, and interconnectedness. These factors were the ground on which creativity could catch fire. The experience of creating together in the same space, with each woman's space respected, led to a sense of individual strength and self-sufficiency.

Working With Fire

In all of the cases which I have described, I can see a connecting thread. The construction of a therapeutic space which can contain, allow and foster free expression is of central importance. In many ways, I can see that it was up to me to provide the intentionality toward such a space: to set the stage, to provide the material, to lay the ground, and then to encourage images to come forth. When I felt the images dry up or the space going dead, I needed to wonder what was happening and to see if an intervention was necessary. There was an ongoing dance with the issue of safety: were we playing it so safe that nothing was happening or was the atmosphere getting too scary because it was too literal—for example, in my work with Angela? Playing with the boundaries between reality and phantasy in paying attention to the *imaginal reality* was a constant factor in the work.

What informs my work in expressive arts therapy is the interplay between the creation of a transitional space, the enlivening of that space by means of the arts, and the movement between myself and the patient which results in the building up of a therapeutic relationship. In work with children, there is the additional factor of the influences of the outside world: family, school, others. Holding all of these elements in mind and seeing how the expression is shaped by the child to involve or not involve all of these elements is a complex and fascinating task. In work with adults, particularly in groups, there is a holding as well and the creation of transitional spaces which maximize freedom of expression. There is also a sense of uncovering in the work—experience has layered over primary creativity and a direct relationship to the self. The arts in therapy have the capacity to help reconnect and recover lost fire in the self.

I believe that focusing on deepening creativity and tending the fire with those whose experience of themselves and of the world has become de-formed helps to stimulate hope. This hope comes from the act of re-forming and re-shaping experience into a new configuration. This new configuration is embodied concretely in a work of art: a dance, a drama, a sculpture, a mask. The art work holds hope and the possibility of more creative fire to come.

Afterword

Playing With Fire: Reflections on the Ethics of Expressive Arts Therapy

If we step back to reflect upon the project of expressive arts therapy, we find that there is an implicit ethics in our work. By ethics, I mean a certain style or way of doing the work. Ethics needs to be distinguished from morality in the sense of a code, a set of rules and prohibitions. Morality distinguishes right and wrong and sets down standards for behaviour. Ethics in its original sense refers to the *ethos* or way of the community. In the current epoch, I am greatly disturbed by the emergence of rigid morality in many quarters of life—from right-wing fundamentalism to left-wing political correctness which has led to its own form of fundamentalism. In these cases, what has happened is the collapse of ethics into morality and the lack of a distinction between the two.

This tendency to claim absolute "truth" has invaded the sphere of therapeutic practice as well. Associations of therapists have developed "codes of ethics" for practitioners. These are misnamed and should be more accurately termed "moral precepts" or "codes of moral behaviour." These codes determine right ways of behaving toward clients and guard against what are termed "boundary crossings." Work with the artistic disciplines, however, shows us that we need to go into the unknown and that crossing boundaries in art is essential work. Therefore, I feel that our work is antithetical to this type of moral code. However, we do need a morality which exists within the framework of an ethical perspective. Morality becomes rigid when it is not informed by an ethical vision. Hopefully, a morality for our work would give us a set of structures that prevent violations of the rights of others while encouraging the expression of their creativity.

What, then, is our ethos as expressive therapists? What are our guiding principles and how are these principles translated into actions? If an ethics shows the way or the appropriate way in which the practice of art-in-therapy is performed, how do we define this? The following is a begining attempt to define our ethics. I hope that this will stimulate a discussion within our community from which we can all learn.

1. We make a distinction between literal reality, imaginal reality, and effective reality.

In the book, *Minstrels of Soul* (1995), Knill, Barba, and Fuchs develop the categories of realities that we work with when we practice a therapy that is rooted in the arts. The distinctions between these levels of psychic reality are critical and are set out as follows:

> Material that emerges from dreams, imagination, fantasies or works of art, then, make up what we call *imaginal reality*. Material that emerges from the so-called actual world, usually referred to as "reality," we will refer to as our *literal reality*. An *effective reality* may be explained also as the experience of engaging in an "I-Thou" relationship, which does not assume objectivity and is distinct from a distancing "I-It" relationship....In an *effective reality,* soul is affected and manifests itself physically and psychologically in a *real* fashion (Knill et al., 1995, p. 62).

When we are working in the discipline of the arts, we know the differences between these levels of reality, and we recognize the borders between them. As expressive arts therapists, we dwell in the imaginal and effective realms; we do not literalize material that is coming from the psyche. The world of metaphors and images does not literally correspond to the real world, although it may draw on residues from literal reality. As artists and therapists, our ethos is to stay in the imaginal and effective realm and to maximize expression coming from these realms. If we are literalizing or taking the messages literally, then we have lost our way. In the context of our way of working, this might be considered a form of unethical practice. It is our task to keep the thoughts and messages in the form of images which are visual, kinesthetic, and auditory. We play with these images, keeping them fresh and multi-dimensional.

It is this commitment to imagination that provides the possibility for change to happen in literal reality. We heighten expression in therapy and crystallize this expression in an artistic form or a series of artistic forms in order to effect change in the lives of our patients. The imaginal creates new possibilites for thinking and action. Paradoxically, the imagination can do its work only when it is carefully distinguished from literal reality.

To literalize in therapy means that we flatten the material, compress and compartmentalize it. We remain one-dimensional. The difference between cognitive/behavioural approaches in therapy and expressive arts therapy makes the point clearer. In the cognitive approach, one operates entirely in literal reality; this is its ethos. One helps the patient modify behaviour in the real world by actually experiencing new behavioural patterns and observing their effect on others' behaviour. Our ethos in expressive arts therapy involves staying in the imaginal and effective realms as much as possible and using the frame of the artistic disciplines in order to effect change.

2. We work with the interplay between safety and risk-taking

Because our ethics clarifies the fact that we dwell in the imaginal realm, it also makes it clear that this is a framed reality which borrows from literal reality but is, at the same time, separate and distinct. Safety is an issue that comes up in our work both in therapy and in training. Our work is highly safe and highly dangerous at the same time. It is framed and set apart from that which is literally real—we work with the dance or the painting or the drama and stay within these frames, and yet, within them, we encourage total freedom of expression. This may mean feeling unsafe at times. Our ethics demands that we hold the frame around these experiences in order to heighten the experience inside the frame and to create the boundary between this artistic expression and everyday life.

Yet there is also the experience of liminality or the blurring of inside and outside. When we located work with the arts in the transitional space, we noted that this was an experience of both me and not-me, a boundary crossing. Art-making demands that one lose safety and journey away from home, not-knowing in advance what will happen. An ethical expressive arts therapist understands the necessity of such a process of confusion and dis-ease. She can serve as a guide and as a witness at the same time, which means that she holds the distinctions (safety) while encouraging deeper and more complex expression (danger).

An ethical expressive arts therapist understands the importance of losing control in order to gain mastery. She provides the right environment for maximum flexibility. The arts ultimately are containers for expression and, in this sense, provide security and safety.

3. We witness the other in a responsible encounter

When we work with the arts in therapy, there is always the element of relationship—between patient and therapist, between self and materials, all within the transitional space, the third element in the relationship. Relationship involves encounter: with the materials, with the images that are arriving, and with the other. The therapist as guide and witness reflects back elements of the relationship and of the images. It is the responsibility of the therapist to witness this process within the artistic frame. This means that the therapist has to have a sense of aesthetic response-ability: caring for the patient by means of caring for the imaginal and effective realities that are embodied in the images. The witness helps to shape the space of the encounter— to provide a space for creation to happen. The witness is not simply a neutral observer but, rather, provides for the experience of something new to happen.

4. Sensitivity is a major aspect of our work

The therapist as guide, observer, and responder uses a high degree of sensitivity to foster the work. A major component of the ethics of expressive arts therapy is sensitivity both to the arts and to other people. An ethics of expressive arts therapy requires that the therapist train her/himself to be highly sensitive on a number of levels: emotionally, intellectually, physically. In order to develop high sensitivity, it is necessary to work with oneself—to make art, to understand oneself, to feel the connection between oneself and material, other people and the world. The sensitivity that predominates in the work of expressive arts therapy is a *bodily knowing*. Work with others in the arts is a knowing which senses where the next step might be. This is an openness to what will emerge, not a pre-determined sense of knowing. In French, *"sens"* means direction as well as meaning. Sensitivity anticipates direction and flow. We are alert to what is happening on many levels, and we encourage a direction to emerge by framing the space and then following the images.

5. We respect and honor the image

Images are at the forefront of our work. We need to pay special attention to the way in which we treat them. We need to be careful not to engage in what has been termed "image abuse" (McNiff, 1987, Levine, 1992) where the image is reduced to a pathological structure or merely serves as an indicator of underlying meanings which surpass the image itself. If we are doing our work, images will surely arrive. Once they begin to enter the therapy space, our job is to follow them and enhance them. The images that arrive infuse the art materials with life and power. We are facilitators of this aliveness, making sure that there is a proper ground for the images to rest on. This task involves keeping imaginal and effective realities primary in the therapy work. It also means that we pay special attention to all the possible pathways that the image might take and become comfortable and familiar with the arts in an interdisciplinary framework. We know that images are not necessarily confined to one or another artistic form.

6. We work with the fire of creativity and keep it burning

An ethics of creativity in therapy makes a deep commitment to the perpetuating of creative spirit and energy in its practice. This is a tricky area and has caused some of the moves toward rigid codes of morality in other styles of psychotherapeutic practice. At its core, creativity taps into the fire of sexuality; work with the arts is deeply connected to the erotic. The aliveness that we feel when we have dropped down into a creative mode has to do with tapping into our erotic life. As therapists who work directly with the fire of creativity, we are bound in our ethics to hold the distinctions between literal, imaginal and effective realities. On the front lines of our work, these are not abstract distinctions.

When therapists confuse these realms, there can be difficulty: if a patient has an erotic transference to the therapist through the work of expressive arts therapy which awakens sleeping eros through artistic expression, the therapist must stay out of the literal realm and avoid confusing literal and imaginal realms. If inevitable feelings of attraction to the patient emerge, these cannot be taken literally and then acted upon. If this happens, ethical practice is derailed, and the container of imaginal reality has been flattened and squashed.

Therapists who work with fire need to be careful of its power to burn out of control. They also need to be aware of the possiblity that the fire will go out. Therefore, an important component of an ethics of our work is the need for therapists to nurture their own fire and keep it burning. This means that we will only be ethical guides when we ourselves engage in art-making and keep in contact with our own creative life. Burn-out, a significant problem for all helpers, is a real danger in our work. Tending to other fires may sometimes mean that we neglect our own.

In this beginning attempt to develop a positive ethics for expressive arts therapy, I have tried to show how we need to have an ethics which is indigenous to our practice. A negative set of prohibitions on behaviour does not suit our work in any way. However, there may be some these days who criticize our work for the risks that it takes and its appearance of lack of safety. Working with the arts in a deep way is not totally safe activity. Although it is framed and set apart from literal reality, art-making still takes chances and goes into the unknown. The question is, can we ever go into painful and confusing places and stay completely safe at the same time?

This question comes up continually in work with those who have survived abuse, particularly sexual abuse and incest. One way to look at abuse is to see that as a result of the abusive situation, the person's sexual energy was de-formed. In incest, the erotic relationship which normally exists between parent and child was *literalized*. It was not playfully enacted but, rather, literally acted-out. Here there was a boundary-crossing which violated the space of the other. As a response to this situation, current trends in ethics have focused on the further literalizing of abuse and have led to the development of sets of prohibitions. This creates an atmosphere in which those who were abused are encouraged to take literal revenge on their abusers, becoming abusers themselves.

Our response to such ethical dilemmas is to show the way of our work. Rather than literalizing the abusive situation in terms of attempting to take revenge, our work enables people to play with their violations through the arts. We can create an imaginal reality which varies and changes the situation. For example, an abused person can have a chance to play the abuser in a drama. While playing with the trauma may lead to mastery and a feeling of control, it is not control in the rigid sense. We still can work with the not-knowing and with the arts which are open-ended and mysterious in terms of what the outcome will be. The goal would be to reconnect with the sexual energy that was violated and to reconnect sexuality with creativity in a positive sense, to re-infuse and reintegrate sexuality into life.

In order to do work of this sort, it is important to trust in the arts to lead the way. If we lead with a rigid set of rules or moral prohibitions, it will mitigate against the very work that we are trying to do. If we have our ethics as guiding principles, on the other hand, we need not be afraid. As artists, we are always playing with fire. We allow ourselves to go into dangerous territory, and often we find pain and suffering there. When we go to these deep places with others, we need to be keepers and tenders of their fire—with sensitivity, response-ability, imagination, and aliveness. Tending the fire is the ethical basis of expressive arts therapy.

Fire

insists its way
into the most minimal
passageways

Nothing here is at rest
Everything leaps and breathes
with some other dancing self

Yes. Many *have* died here
Some didn't come back. Some did.
It was a question of the heat's
intensity. And timing.

At one point
the flames took over
everything. There was no going
anywhere but
Red.

The animals baffled were led from the barn.
The birds in terror fled from the forest.

All I remembered
afterwards was the soft
touch of ash. Where there *had*
been land. Where the trees had sighed
and produced fruit.

Bonfires every-
where. And the small
sounds of birds gasping
uncommonly. In the common

smoke.

My smoke
is in your fire

Your fire
is in my forest

My forest
is on your land

Your land
is on my boundary

My boundary
is on your frontier

Your frontier
is on my shoreline

My shoreline
is in your water

Your water is in my air
My air is in your breath

Your breath is in my song   my song is in your
heart   your heart is in my blood   my
blood is in your hands   your
hands are on my body   my body
is on your mind   your
mind is in my spirit
my spirit is in your fire   your fire
is in my life   my life

is in your hands
your hands are in my love
my love is in your life

your life is in my life
My life. My life
Is on fire

Elizabeth Gordon McKim

BIBLIOGRAPHY

Bachelard, Gaston. (1964). *The Psychoanalysis of Fire*. Boston: The Beacon Press.

Freud, Sigmund. (1955). *Beyond the Pleasure Principle*. In *The Standard Edition of the Complete Psychological Works of Sigmund Freud*. Volume 18. Ed. and Trans. James Strachey. London: Hogarth Press and the Institute of Psychoanalysis.

_____. (1955). *Three Essays on the Theory of Sexuality*. In *The Standard Edition of the Complete Psychological Works of Sigmund Freud*. Volume 7. Ed. and Trans. James Strachey. London: Hogarth Press and the Institute of Psychoanalysis.

Klein, Melanie. (1975 A). *Love, Guilt and Reparation and Other Works*. (1921-1945). London: Hogarth Press and the Institute of Psychoanalysis.

_____. (1975 B). *Envy and Gratitude and Other Works*. (1946-1963). London: Hogarth Press and the Institute of Psychoanalysis.

Knill, Paolo, Barba, Helen, N. and Fuchs, Margot N. (1995). *Minstrels of Soul: Intermodal Expressive Therapy*. Toronto: Palmerston Press.

Levine, Ellen G. (1989). "Women and Creativity: Art-In-Relationship." *The Arts in Psychotherapy*. Volume 16.

Levine, Stephen K. (1992). *Poiesis: The Language of Psychology and the Speech of the Soul*. Toronto: Palmerston Press.

McNiff, Shaun. (1992). *Art as Medicine*. Boston: Shambhala Press.

Robbins, Arthur. (1987). *The Artist as Therapist.* New York: Human Sciences Press, Inc.

Rogers, Natalie. (1993). *The Creative Connection: Expressive Arts as Healing.* Palo Alto: Science and Behavior Books.

Segal, Hannah. (1973). *Introduction to the Work of Melanie Klein.* London: The Hogarth Press and the Institute of Psychoanalysis.

Waller, Diane. (1993). *Group Interactive Art Therapy.* London: Routledge.

Watkins, Mary. (1981). "Six Approaches to the Image in Art Therapy." *Spring.*

Winnicott, D.W. (1965). *The Maturational Processes and the Facilitating Environment.* New York: International Universities Press.

_____. (1971). *Playing and Reality.* London: Penguin Books.

_____. (1971). *Therapeutic Consultations in Child Psychiatry.* London: The Hogarth Press.

_____. (1975). *Collected Papers: Through Paediatrics to Psycho-Analysis.* London: The Hogarth Press.